THE ABINGDON WORSHIP ANNUAL

2004

CONTEMPORARY & TRADITIONAL
RESOURCES FOR WORSHIP LEADERS

ABINGDON
WORSHIP
Annual
2004

EDITED BY MARY J. SCIFRES & B. J. BEU
FOREWORD BY BRIAN WREN

Abingdon Press
Nashville

THE ABINGDON WORSHIP ANNUAL 2004
CONTEMPORARY AND TRADITIONAL RESOURCES
FOR WORSHIP LEADERS

Copyright © 2003 by Abingdon Press

This book is printed on recycled, acid-free, elemental-chlorine–free paper.

ISBN 0-687-063264-01

All scripture quotations unless noted otherwise are taken from the *New Revised Standard
Version of the Bible,* copyright © 1989, Division of Christian Education of the National
Council of the Churches of Christ in the United States of America. Used by permission.
All rights reserved.

Scripture quotations noted (REB) are from the Revised English Bible © Oxford
University Press and Cambridge University Press 1989.

Selections by Mark Stamm are © Mark Stamm. Used by permission.

Selections by Brian Wren are © Brian Wren. Used by permission.

03 04 05 06 07 08 09 10 11 12—10 9 8 7 6 5 4 3 2 1
MANUFACTURED IN THE UNITED STATES OF AMERICA

CONTENTS

105497

OCTOBER

NOVEMBER

DECEMBER

FOREWORD

"Sweepers of the Spirit's Way"
by Brian Wren

Not long ago, a student described a worship service he attended. It followed the congregation's customary pattern: songs of praise, prayer, one passage of scripture, to which the pastor's sermon gave lengthy and detailed exposition, a closing hymn, and a benediction. Somewhere, an offering was taken.

For the congregation in question, and for its pastor, the purpose of worship is to prepare the way for preaching, the purpose of preaching is to teach the meaning of scripture, and the purpose of reading scripture is to present the basis of the sermon. If anything else happens—if, for example, Christ speaks and the Spirit moves among the worshipers as scripture is read, prayers are offered, and songs are sung—it is a bonus, even perhaps a distraction.

For the publishers and editors of this book, and its contributors, every part of worship is a gateway for God's glory. Though *The Abingdon Worship Annual* focuses on words—or rather on worship speech, words crafted for utterance—it does not stand alone, but takes its place on the bookshelf alongside resources for preaching, song, drama, visuals, dance, and other worship arts.

To set the scene for what might happen when we take this book off the shelf, open it, and plan upcoming worship, here are some thoughts about worship leadership and design, based on, and interspersed with, verses of the hymn, "How Great the Mystery of Faith!" Worship deals with awesome mysteries, but happens so regularly that worship planning must become a matter of priorities, deadlines, and routines. In the midst of our planning, it behooves us to pause, take a cue from 1 Timothy 3:15, and whisper:

> How great the mystery of faith,
> how deep the purposes of God,
> in birth and aging, life and death,
> unveiled, yet never understood!

Every word in this *Annual* reaches for that mystery; everything falls short; and at every stage in our planning, from midweek meditation to Saturday night desperation, we imagine our congregation's probable longing as worship begins:

> Attracted by life's deepest claim
> we wait, assembled in this place,
> with needs and hopes we cannot name,
> athirst for healing, truth and grace.

Decades ago, I did compulsory military service. The "character forming" disciplines of army life included applying weekly coats of whitewash to parade ground boundary stones, peeling hundreds of potatoes by hand, and sweeping the barrack-room floor.

Sweeping was (and is) unexpectedly satisfying. It is a menial occupation, and (if you do it for a living) very poorly paid. Yet to sweep a room successfully calls for planning, application, and concentration. Worship planning, and the preparation of worship speech, is like sweeping a way for the Spirit of God. It is artful, yet humble, and when we are done, we step back, and wait in hope:

> The best that we can do and say,
> the utmost care of skill and art,

are sweepers of the Spirit's way
to reach the depths of every heart.

So it is that, when planning ends, worship begins with
prayer:

Come, walk among us, Holy Friend,
as all are gathered and prepared,
that scattered lives may meet and mend
through open Word and table shared.*

---

*Brian Wren is the Conant Professor of Worship at Columbia Theological
Seminary, Decatur, Georgia, and a Minister of the United Reformed
Church (UK). The hymn, "How Great the Mystery of Faith!" is from his
anthology, *Piece Together Praise—a Theological Journey: Poems and Collected
Hymns Thematically Arranged* (Carol Stream, Ill.: Hope Publishing
Company, 1996). The text of the hymn is copyright © 1989 by Hope
Publishing Company, Carol Stream, IL 60199. All rights reserved.
Reprinted by permission. This foreword is copyright © 2002 by Brian
Wren.

INTRODUCTION

This new book in Abingdon's long line of worship and preaching resources fills a void in most pastors' and worship planners' libraries. While worship resources abound, few provide sufficient breadth and scope to design coherent and coordinated worship experiences for both traditional and contemporary worship. *The Abingdon Worship Annual* addresses this need. In it, you will find suggestions for each Sunday of the year (and most holy days) to help plan your corporate worship services. Although space did not permit us to include every worship idea from our contributing authors, this book offers what we believe to be the most commonly used and most needed worship resources. Each entry includes: Calls to Worship, Opening Prayers, Praise Sentences or Contemporary Gathering Words, Prayers of Confession or Unison Prayers, and Benedictions or Closing Prayers.

The Abingdon Worship Annual was written to complement *The Abingdon Preaching Annual*. In addition, the *Abingdon Worship Annual* can be used with *Prepare! A Weekly Worship Planbook for Pastors and Musicians* or *The United Methodist Music and Worship Planner*. As pastors, we recognize that few pastors have as much time and creative energy to spend planning their services of worship as they would like. Despite our best intentions, heavy counseling loads, unexpected deaths and illnesses, crises within the congregation, or pressing administrative responsibilities often limit the time we are able to spend on any given Sunday service. Just as *Prepare!* and *The United Methodist Music and Worship Planner* are tremendous time-savers, containing hymn and keyboard suggestions, vocal solos, anthem suggestions, and contemporary musical suggestions, *The Abingdon Worship Annual* provides pastors and worship planners the liturgical elements to put a complete service of worship together. As you design your worship service, we invite you to read through the scriptures for each day. Then read through the liturgical suggestions in this resource that speak to those readings. Use this resource as the Spirit guides you, letting God's word flow through you and the members of your worship planning team. Trust God's guidance, and enjoy a wonderful year of worship and praise with your congregation! As you do so, here are a few ideas to consider.

Worship leaders sometimes omit the rubrics (or instructions) that congregations need to feel at ease as they negotiate the intricate maze of modern worship. Don't hesitate to begin a Prayer or Call to Worship by offering simple instructions, such as:

Please join in the Call to Worship.

Let us worship God as we speak together.

Let us praise God.

Please pray with me.

Let us pray together.

Let us come to Jesus Christ, confessing our sin and our need.

Please join me in praising God.

Remember that body language communicates as effectively as verbal language. Raise your arms as you invite those who are able to stand. Bow your head (keeping close to the microphone) as you invite others to pray with you. Smile and speak energetically when offering Words of Praise! Most of all, worship God as you invite others to do so. As we lead the people of God in worship, the congregation needs to experience the authenticity of our love for God.

As you work with the 2004 edition of the *Worship Annual*, some comments may be helpful in using it to the fullest. Calls to Worship are words that gather God's people together as they prepare to worship God. Often called "Greetings" or "Gathering Words," these words are typically read responsively. Some of the Contemporary Gathering Words listed under each entry may also be helpful as Calls to Worship in a traditional or blended setting. As with all responsive readings, think creatively as you plan your services. While it is simplest to have a single leader read the words in light print, with the congregation responding by reading the words in bold print, it is often effective to have several people, or even groups of people, lead these calls. Using the choir, a youth group, or a small prayer group adds variety and vitality to your services. Some congregations enjoy responding to one another: women to men, right side to left side, children to parents. Experiment with a variety of options, and see how these words might be most meaningful in calling your congregation together to worship the Holy One.

Contemporary Gathering Words and Praise Sentences are offered here to assist pastors and worship leaders who are new to the art of leading less formal worship, sometimes called "Contemporary Worship." Leaders who find speaking extemporaneously difficult will find these entries particularly helpful when leading worship.

Like more formal Calls to Worship, Gathering Words are often read responsively. Unlike more formal Calls to Worship, however, Gathering Words tend to use simpler language and be more repetitive in nature. You may copy these Gathering Words onto an overhead transparency to help your congregation read responsively without being tied to a bulletin. If your congregation does not care to read words aloud, consider using two leaders to speak in "call and response" format. Or, allow the song team or band members to act as responders to the worship leader, echoing the call and response tradition of African American Christians.

While many of the Praise Sentences provided in this resource are easily spoken by one leader, using the call and response format is an option. In praise settings, worshipers are often willing to respond in echo form, repeating the words or phrases spoken by the worship leader. Echoing the same words and phrases several times can be highly effective. The Praise Sentences in this resource are not intended to limit you, but rather to free you to lead in a more informal style where appropriate.

Opening Prayers in this resource are varied in form, but typically invoke God's presence in worship. Some are more informal than others, and some are more general than formal invocations. Many can be adapted for use later in the worship service, if that suits your needs. For the sake of simplicity, we have grouped them all into the category of "Opening Prayers."

Prayers of Confession and Words of Assurance follow many different formats. At times, the "Assurance of Pardon" is actually contained in the prayer. When it is not, you may wish to use Words of Assurance from a previous day's suggested resources or from a favorite scripture of assurance. Some scriptures, particularly in the Easter season, do not lend themselves to confession and, thus, such prayers are absent.

Prayers take many forms in this resource. Some are in the form of a Collect. Prayers need not be spoken in unison, but may be spoken alone by a single leader or led by a small group. Some prayers may even be adapted as Opening or Closing Prayers. They may be revised into call and response format. In all cases, we have sought to provide words that can easily be spoken by a large congregation in unison. For the sake of consistency, such entries have been given the title, "Unison Prayer." You may use any title you deem appropriate in your worship bulletin.

Litanies or Responsive Readings offer additional ways of speaking together in worship. Certain scriptures and themes elicited such provocative Litanies that we had to include them. We hope you will find this a helpful addition. Again, think creatively as you decide how these Responsive

Readings are read in your service of worship: whether in unison, by a worship leader alone, or in a call and response format.

Benedictions, sometimes known as "Blessings" or "Words of Dismissal," are included in each entry. Some work best in call and response format; others seem more appropriate as a solitary blessing from the worship leader. Choose a format best suited to your congregation: whether in unison, by a worship leader alone, or in a call and response format.

This is our first year of publishing *The Abingdon Worship Annual.* Please let us hear from you as you work with this resource. In future volumes, we hope to integrate your ideas on improving this resource while maintaining those features that are most helpful to you. We are eager to learn what does and does not work for you.

Enjoy this resource, and enjoy the year ahead. We wish you God's blessings as you seek to share Christ's word and offer experiences of the Spirit in your work and worship!

MARY J. SCIFRES AND B. J. BEU

JANUARY 1, 2004

Watch Night/New Year
B. J. Beu

COLOR
White

SCRIPTURE READINGS
Ecclesiastes 3:1-13; Psalm 8; Revelation 21:1-6a; Matthew 25:31-46

THEME IDEAS
This is a time for reflection and anticipation. Rather than judging the past year by how happy or successful we were, God reminds us that weeping, tearing down, and lying fallow are all part of the seasons and rhythms of life. The true barometer of our lives comes from how we treat the living Christ: by feeding the hungry, clothing the naked, visiting the sick and imprisoned, and comforting those who mourn. As we look with anticipation to the new year, we place our trust in the One whose glory is beheld in the new heaven and new earth—the One who will wipe away every tear.

CALL TO WORSHIP (ECCLESIASTES 3)
God creates the seasons of our lives.
Thanks be to God!
In seasons of rejoicing, we do not laugh alone.
Thanks be to God!

In seasons of mourning, we do not weep alone.
Thanks be to God!
When we sow and when we reap, we are not alone.
Thanks be to God!
We worship the One who holds our past, present, and future.
Thanks be to God!

CALL TO WORSHIP (PSALM 8)

O God, you are wonderful, how majestic is your name!
We behold your glory in the heavens!
What are human beings that you are mindful of us?
What are mortals that you care for us?
Yet you create us in your image.
We behold your glory in one another.
You entreat us to care for your creatures.
We behold your glory in the works of your hands.
O God, you are wonderful, how majestic is your name!

CALL TO WORSHIP (MATTHEW 25)

Christ is the Good Shepherd, protector of God's sheep.
Christ calls us into God's flock and watches over us.
Christ rewards our faithful service with the gift of eternal life.
Because we belong to the Shepherd, we rest secure in God's love.

CONTEMPORARY GATHERING WORDS (ECCLESIASTES 3)

God brings us to a new year.
Rejoice and be glad!
God brings us to new seasons of joy and hope.
Rejoice and be glad!
God shares our pain in seasons of sadness and loss.
Rejoice and be glad!

God desires that we enjoy our lives.
Rejoice and be glad!

PRAISE SENTENCES (PSALM 8)
God's name is above all names.
The works of God are a wonder to behold.
God fills us with glory. Praise God's holy name!

OPENING PRAYER (REVELATION 21)
O God our hope,
  in you we see the promise of a new heaven and new
  earth.
You dwell among us and call us to be your people.
May our lives reflect the wonder of your presence.
May our actions be worthy of the One who wipes away
  every tear,
    that others may lift their eyes and behold your glory.
We pray this in name of the Alpha and the Omega,
  the first and the last, Jesus Christ our Lord. Amen.

OPENING PRAYER (NEW YEAR)
Eternal God,
  foundation of all that is, and was, and is to be,
  bless us as we come to a new year.
Help us forgive ourselves for our past failings,
  and open our eyes to possibilities that lie before us.
Guide our footsteps,
  that the coming year may bring the joy
  of your presence to those we meet. Amen.

OPENING PRAYER (PSALM 8)
Great Spirit, Light of all light, and Truth of all truth,
  your care is beheld in all creation.
We behold your power in the mighty waters of the sea.
We see your beauty in the fair flowers of the meadow,
  and in the deep forest green.

Your strength fills the lion and the bear with power.
And the glory of your image shines forth in your people.
Open our eyes,
    that we may see our connection with all living things.
Open our hearts,
    that we may reach out to one another,
    for we are all part of one great family. Amen.

PRAYER OF CONFESSION (MATTHEW 25)
Holy God,
    we have not always loved you as we ought.
We praise you with our lips,
    yet we are silent about those who are hungry
    and want for clothing.
We lift up our eyes to behold your glory,
    but we turn our gaze away from the homeless
    and the needy.
Forgive us Lord,
    when we are quicker to proclaim our faith in you,
    than we are to live that faith.
Help us to think of the welfare of others
    as often as we think of our own welfare,
    that we might hear our names called among the faithful,
    when you come again in glory. Amen.

BENEDICTION (ECCLESIASTES 3)
Every season in life is a blessing from God.
We rejoice in God's blessings!
Every purpose under heaven is part of God's plan.
We rejoice in God's blessings!
God wishes us to be happy and fulfilled.
We rejoice in God's blessings!

JANUARY 4, 2004

Second Sunday After Christmas
Mary J. Scifres

COLOR
White

SCRIPTURE READINGS
Jeremiah 31:7-14; Psalm 147:12-20; Ephesians 1:3-14; John 1:(1-9) 10-18

THEME IDEAS
God's Word, Christ's glory, and our grace-filled adoption as God's children arise as common themes throughout today's readings. As the new year begins, such images can bring inspiration stronger than our wavering resolution to live our faith. As children of God, people are given the opportunity to live in the presence of Christ's glory, and walk alongside God's Word. Glory to God in the Highest!

CALL TO WORSHIP AND OPENING PRAYER (JOHN 1)
In the beginning was the Word,
and the Word was with God.
All things came into being through the Word,
and the Word was with God.
In Christ, the Word, light and life came into being,
and the Word was with God.

In Christ, the Word, light overcame darkness,
and the Word was with God.
So in this time of worship, may Christ be with us,
light overcoming darkness, life overcoming death.
Come, Christ the Word, be with us as we worship.

CONTEMPORARY GATHERING WORDS (JEREMIAH 31)

Sing with gladness, all God's people.
We come, singing God's praise!
Sing with gladness, all God's people.
We come, singing God's praise!
Sing with gladness, all God's people.
We come, singing God's praise!

PRAISE SENTENCES (PSALM 147)

Praise our mighty God of strength!
Praise our peaceful God of love!
Praise God, who sends the Word into our lives!

OPENING PRAYER (JEREMIAH 31)

Gather us together, Shepherding God. Comfort us as we
reflect on the sorrows of the past year. Rejoice with us as
we remember times of gladness. Dance with us in this
time of worship, that we may know you and you may be
our God. Amen.

PRAYER OF CONFESSION (JOHN 1)

Christ of Light and Life,
 we pray for your forgiveness this day.
For the times when we do not know you,
 forgive us.
For the days when we do not see your light shining,
 forgive us.
For the ways in which we do not receive you,
 forgive us.

For the situations in which we have not used our power
to be children of God,
forgive us.
Guide us, we pray, to see your glory, full of grace and truth.
In your life-giving name, we pray. Amen.

WORDS OF ASSURANCE (JOHN 1)
Children of God,
Christ has poured grace upon grace over us.
Receive Christ's grace in all its fullness,
and know that you are forgiven.

PRAYER FOR JUSTICE (JEREMIAH 31)
Save us from ourselves, O Lord,
when we neglect your call in our lives.
Guide us on your path of justice and love.
Bring us into unity with one another
and with those we call "other."
Whether blind or full of vision;
whether limping or running;
whether barren or surrounded by children;
whether first or last,
let us remember that we are yours. Amen.

BENEDICTION
God has sent the Word to us.
We go out as the Word to a world in need.
God has given us grace upon grace.
We go out as grace to a world in need.
God has given us light and life through Christ Jesus.
**We go out as Christ's instruments of light and life
to a world in need.**
May it be so.
Amen.

JANUARY 6, 2004

Epiphany of the Lord
Mary J. Scifres

COLOR
White

SCRIPTURE READINGS
Isaiah 60:1-6; Psalm 72:1-7, 10-14; Ephesians 3:1-12; Matthew 2:1-12

THEME IDEAS
The light of Christ's grace, God's loving brightness, and the Holy Spirit's wisdom and guidance are all symbolized in the star followed by the sages of old in this morning's lesson from Matthew. The meaning of light is a promise of hope in the midst of darkness, particularly as the "blah" days of January follow the bright Christmas lights of December. The meaning of light is a promise of guidance through the dark days of winter. This Sunday is a Sunday to celebrate that light and lift up the promise that Christ's light brings into a new year, and into a cold, dreary winter month.

CALL TO WORSHIP (ISAIAH 60)
Arise, shine!
  God's light has come!
Arise, shine!
  Christ has been born!

Arise, shine!
God's glory is all around!
Arise, shine!
We come to worship the God of Glory!
Glory to God in the highest!
And on earth, peace!

CALL TO WORSHIP (EPHESIANS 3, MATTHEW 2)

Let us gather together to worship the Christ child.
We come to experience the mystery.
Let us bow before God, offering our gifts and our love.
We come to revel in the riches of God's grace.
Let us open our hearts and our minds to God's Holy Spirit.
We come to know the wisdom and the purpose that brings us to this place.
Come, let us gather together to worship the Christ child.
We have come!
Let us gather together to worship our God.

CONTEMPORARY GATHERING WORDS (ISAIAH 60, MATTHEW 2)

Come into God's presence.
Christ's light is shining on us!
Christ's light is shining!
Christ's light is shining!
Christ's light is shining!
We have come to sing God's praises.
Christ's light shines all around us!

PRAISE SENTENCES (PSALM 72)

God will defend and deliver us in all adversity!
Christ will stand up for us and save us when we are defeated.
Because of God's love, we never face difficulties alone!
Praise God for the grace and abundant love that saves us!

PRAISE SENTENCES (ISAIAH 60)
Christ is our light. There is no darkness, for the light has come! Praise God for Christ's light!

OPENING PRAYER (EPIPHANY)
God of light and love,
    come to us this day.
Shine upon us,
    that we might know your presence more fully.
Shine within us,
    that we might live your truth more freely.
Shine around us,
    that we might know your world of love and grace.
In the name of your brightest light,
    Christ Jesus, we pray.
Amen.

OPENING PRAYER (NEW YEAR)
God of new beginnings,
    we come into your presence
    asking for new life and hope.
Let this time of worship be a time of rebirth,
    of hope born anew.
As we open our hearts and our lives to you,
    fill us with your Holy Spirit,
    that our hearts and our lives might be more Christlike
    with each new day. Amen.

PRAYER OF CONFESSION (PSALM 72)
Grant us your justice, O God,
    for we come on this first Sunday of the new year
    aware that our world is full of injustice.
Grant us your justice, Loving One,
    for we offer this prayer,
    aware that our hearts are too often full of injustice.
Judge us with righteousness and kindness,

for we are your people.
May your love and your light shine upon us,
    and upon our world in this new year. Amen.

BENEDICTION

May we go forth,
sharing our prosperity with all people.
    Let Christ's light shine through us!
May we go forth,
offering justice and righteousness in all our actions.
    Let Christ's light shine through us!
May we go forth,
caring for the poor and the needy.
    Let Christ's light shine through us!
May God's love fall like rain upon us,
that our love may fall upon the world,
like a gentle snow and a strong shower.
    Let Christ's light shine through us!

JANUARY 11, 2004

First Sunday After the Epiphany/Baptism of the Lord

Mark W. Stamm

COLOR
White

SCRIPTURE READINGS
Isaiah 43:1-7; Psalm 29; Acts 8:14-17; Luke 3:15-17, 21-22

THEME IDEAS
Baptism of the Lord Sunday provides an excellent opportunity for baptisms and congregational reaffirmation of the baptismal covenant. In the baptismal covenant, we celebrate God's gift of the Spirit, our adoption into God's family, and the call to discipleship. Let these themes interact dynamically. Don't just talk about water, but use it, and plenty of it. Let the congregation see water, hear it, feel it, and touch it. Baptize lavishly.

CALL TO WORSHIP (LUKE 3, ACTS 8, ISAIAH 43)
Remember your baptism! Jesus came among sinners and was baptized, like each of us.
Alleluia! Thanks be to God!
Remember your baptism! Jesus received the Holy Spirit, which he shares with us.
Alleluia! Thanks be to God!

Remember your baptism! Jesus calls us by name, and will never let us go.
Alleluia! Thanks be to God!

CONTEMPORARY GATHERING WORDS (ACTS 8, LUKE 3)

Perhaps you hear the words
"Remember your baptism and be thankful,"
and you realize: "I don't remember a thing."
You are not alone.
Like many of you, I don't remember my baptism,
and I'm still trying to figure out what baptism means.
But, here's what I do know:
Baptism is about what Jesus is doing in our midst.
Baptism is about the work of God's Spirit
in my life and in our life together.
Baptism is about God's promises and God's call.
Baptism is a mystery deeper than I can fathom;
yet this mystery is rooted in God's love.
So let us worship God and explore the mystery together.

OPENING PRAYER (ACTS 8, LUKE 3)

Mighty and merciful God,
you claim us in baptism,
and bestow the gift of the Holy Spirit—
the same Spirit you gave Jesus at his baptism.
Fill us with this Spirit,
that as we love you and serve you
with joy and courage,
we may walk with Jesus. Amen.

PRAYER OF CONFESSION (BASED ON "THE BAPTISMAL COVENANT I")

Merciful God,
you receive us in baptism and claim us as your own.
Yet we confess that we have not kept this covenant.

We have not repented of our sin.
We have not rejected evil.
We have resisted your Spirit.
We have not confessed Jesus as Lord,
    and we have neglected the means of grace.
We have not nurtured one another,
    and we have not professed the faith of the church.
In spite of our failure, you remain faithful.
Forgive us and renew us in this covenant,
    that we may be faithful disciples of Jesus Christ,
    rejoicing in the power of the Holy Spirit. Amen.

BIDDING PRAYERS, FOR INTERCESSIONS

I ask your prayers for all disciples of Jesus Christ,
    especially for those whom we baptize today.
(silence)
I ask your prayers for all those who prepare for confirmation and the reaffirmation of their baptismal covenant.
(silence)
I ask your prayers for baptismal sponsors and godparents, for pastors, spiritual guides, catechists, and mentors.
(silence)
I ask your prayers for all those who seek God,
    and for those who share the gospel with them.
(silence)
I ask your prayers for all people in any kind of need or trouble, and for those who minister to them.
(silence)

UNISON PRAYER (ISAIAH 43)

God of Creation,
    whose mercy is beyond all that we can imagine,

do not overwhelm us in the deep waters of judgment
and trial.
Stand by us, and deliver us,
that we may praise you in that great congregation
gathered from every land.
We ask this in the name of Jesus Christ our Redeemer,
who with you and the Holy Spirit,
lives and reigns, one God, now and forever.
Amen.

BENEDICTION

Friends, you belong to Christ.
Amen. We are baptized!
You are baptized,
anointed by the Spirit for the work of ministry.
Amen. God is with us!
Go forth to love and serve God.
The grace of our Lord Jesus Christ,
the love of God,
and the communion of the Holy Spirit,
be with you now and always.
Amen! Thanks be to God.

VISUAL SUGGESTIONS

Place the baptismal font where all can see it. If it can be
moved to the center of the chancel, do so. Place a large,
clear glass pitcher of water on a stand beside the font. At
the service of the baptismal covenant, pour that water
into the font. Resist the temptation to speak while you
pour. Let the sacramental action speak for itself.

Copyright © Mark W. Stamm, 2002

JANUARY 18, 2004

Second Sunday After the Epiphany
B. J. Beu

COLOR
Green

SCRIPTURE READINGS
Isaiah 62:1-5; Psalm 36:5-10; 1 Corinthians 12:1-11; John 2:1-11

THEME IDEAS
The scriptures illustrate God's sheer delight in, and love for, God's people and all of creation. While God seeks to redeem and be reconciled with Israel, God's salvation extends to animals and to the land itself. Moreover, we are to celebrate the variety of ways in which the people of God are blessed with their own spiritual gifts. Since all gifts come from the same Spirit, we are to treasure one another's gifts. In the Gospel of John, Jesus' first miracle, turning water into wine at a wedding celebration, was both a sign of his messiahship and an act of hospitality. Just as Jesus needed prodding from his mother to use this gift, we often need the prodding of others to use the gifts that God has given us.

CALL TO WORSHIP (PSALM 36)
Your steadfast love, O Lord, extends to the heavens,
your faithfulness to the clouds.

Your righteousness, O Lord, is like the mighty
mountains,
>   **your judgments are like the great deep.**

You save humans and animals alike, O Lord.
>   **How precious is your steadfast love, O God!**

All people take refuge in the shadow of your wings.
>   **They feast on the abundance of your house,**
>   **and you give them drink from the river of your**
>   **delights.**

For with you is the fountain of life.
>   **In your light we see light.**

O continue your steadfast love to those who know you,
>   **and your salvation to the upright of heart!**

CALL TO WORSHIP (1 CORINTHIANS 12)

There are many gifts, but one Spirit.
>   **There are many services, but one Lord.**

We offer our gifts in the service of the living Christ.
>   **We offer our gifts in the service of all God's people.**

CONTEMPORARY GATHERING WORDS (JOHN 2)

Joyful Christ, you transformed water into wine at a
wedding in Cana.
>   **You are greatly to be praised!**

Loving Christ, you are here to transform our hearts of
stone.
>   **You are greatly to be praised!**

Living Christ, you are here in our midst.
>   **You are greatly to be praised!**

PRAISE SENTENCES (PSALM 36)

O God, your love surrounds us. Your faithfulness shields
us. In your light we see light.

PRAISE SENTENCES (ISAIAH 62)

O God, your love shines like the dawn.
>   **Your salvation beckons like a burning torch.**

35

Be our true light.
Crown us with your glory.

OPENING PRAYER (1 CORINTHIANS 12, JOHN 2)

Divine Spirit,
> you come into our world and turn our expectations
> upside down.

We often feel ourselves ill equipped to be Christ's faith-
> ful disciples, yet you bestow upon us your spiritual
> gifts.

We often feel overwhelmed by the demands of life,
> yet you are there to transform the everydayness of our
> lives into moments of celebration.

Just as you changed water into wine at the wedding in
> Cana, you transform our weaknesses into possibilities
> for witness and ministry.

Continue to bless and embolden us,
> that we may not be afraid to help others find their own
> spiritual gifts, and their own moments of wonder.

Amen.

OPENING PRAYER

Spirit of God, your presence is made known in every
> land.

You are revered from mountaintop to the sea.

You are worshiped in the east and in the west,
> in the north and in the south.

Help your people everywhere
> look past the differences that separate us,
> to the gifts of your Sprit that unite us.

When we look at one another,
> help us see not a stranger to be mistrusted,
> but a sister or brother to be embraced.

May the Spirit of Christ, which seeks to make us one,
> guide our hearts and minds into the fullness of your
> grace, through Jesus Christ, our Lord. Amen.

PRAYER OF CONFESSION (1 CORINTHIANS 12)

Gracious God,
> you bestow gifts of the Spirit upon each of us
> to support the common good.

We confess that we have not always recognized
> or valued the gifts that we have received.

We have not always celebrated the gifts given to others,
> nor have we always thought of the common good
> when we use your gifts.

Forgive our failure of vision.

Forgive our pettiness of heart.

And forgive both our self-centeredness and our self-
> neglect.

We know that the One who turned water into wine
> can turn our hearts of stone into hearts of love and
> appreciation.

Thanks be to the living God who makes all things new!
Amen.

BENEDICTION (ISAIAH 62)

God's love shines on us like the dawn.
We are richly blessed!
God's salvation burns in our hearts like a torch.
We are richly blessed!
God rejoices over us, as a bridegroom rejoices over his
bride.
We are richly blessed!

BENEDICTION (PSALM 36)

Let us go forth with God's steadfast love.
We go forth as God's beloved!
Let us go forth to drink from the river of God's delight.
We go forth to drink our fill!
Go forth with God's blessings!

JANUARY 25, 2004

Third Sunday After the Epiphany
Mary J. Scifres

COLOR
Green

SCRIPTURE READINGS
Nehemiah 8:1-3, 5-6, 8-10; Psalm 19; 1 Corinthians 12:12-31*a*; Luke 4:14-21

THEME IDEAS
Although the readings of the Ordinary Season following Epiphany are not woven together in a single theme, several images come to mind today and throughout this season: calling, ministry, law, discipleship, and unity. Nehemiah offers a word of hope and a call to praise, especially for those who know that they fall short in following God's guidance or obeying God's law. The psalmist echoes Nehemiah's call to praise with a reminder that even the heavens, without a voice, can sing God's glory. The call to ministry in Paul's letter to Corinth is intertwined with a call to unity, and Jesus proclaims his own calling and ministry in the Gospel of Luke. Calling, ministry, law, discipleship, and unity—images in this season's readings—are some of the richest and most prevalent themes of the Christian life.

CALL TO WORSHIP (NEHEMIAH 8)
This day is holy to the Lord our God.
Let it be a holy day to us.

This place is holy to the Lord our God.
Let it be a holy place for us.
This moment is a holy moment to the Lord our God.
Let it be a holy moment for us.
Let us come together in worship, making this day, this place, this moment holy for all. Amen.

CALL TO WORSHIP (1 CORINTHIANS 12, PSALM 19)

Christ calls us as one body into worship.
Let the words of our mouths be acceptable.
Christ calls us as one church into worship.
Let the thoughts of our minds be acceptable.
Christ calls us with one Spirit into worship.
Let the meditations of our hearts be acceptable.
Christ calls us with grace and mercy.
Thanks be to God, our Rock and our Redeemer!

CALL TO WORSHIP (PSALM 19)

The heavens are telling of God's glory.
The earth proclaims God's handiwork!
Day and night return endlessly, showing God's steadfast love.
The sun shines upon the earth, reflecting God's light.
Yet even the glory of God's creation cannot outshine God's Word.
The Word of God is a light on our path.
We gather together to study that word and brighten that light.
We gather together to worship God.

CONTEMPORARY GATHERING WORDS (LUKE 4)

The Spirit of the Lord is upon us.
We will hear God's good news!
The Spirit of the Lord is upon us.
We will speak God's good news!

The Spirit of the Lord is upon us.
We will live God's good news!

PRAISE SENTENCES (NEHEMIAH 8:10)

The joy of the Lord is our strength.
The joy of the Lord is our strength!
The joy of the Lord is our strength.
The joy of the Lord is our strength!
Thanks be to God!

OPENING PRAYER (NEHEMIAH 8, 1 CORINTHIANS 12)

God of creation and law,
    we come to you with awe and reverence.
As we enter into this time of worship,
    strengthen us with your power.
Overcome our tears of sorrow and shame
    with the joy of your grace and love.
Let your Spirit guide us in this time together
    and in the days to come,
    that we may be of one Spirit and one mind.
Strong Rock and Gracious Redeemer,
    bind us together as one body in worship of you.
Amen.

PRAYER OF PREPARATION (PSALM 19:14)

Our Rock and our Redeemer,
    let the words spoken this morning be your words.
Let the thoughts and meditation of our hearts and minds
    be pleasing to you.
Let this time of reflection on your word
    bring strength and redemption to our lives. Amen.

PRAYER OF RESPONSE (PSALM 19)

O Lord, our God, let us hear your perfect word
    that your teachings may revive our souls.

Let us live your law,
   that our days may be filled with simple wisdom.
Amen.

RESPONSIVE PRAYER (1 CORINTHIANS 12)
   In the one Spirit, we are all baptized.
   Lord, make us one.
   We are called to be one in the Spirit.
   Lord, make us one.
   We are all members of the body of Christ.
   Lord, make us one.
   We are called to be one in Christ Jesus.
   Lord, make us one.
   When one of us suffers, we are all called to suffer.
   Lord, make us one.
   When one of us rejoices, we are all called to rejoice.
   Lord, make us one.
   Christ of compassion, Spirit of unity
   bind us together as one,
   that we might truly be your body
   in ministry to the world.
   Amen.

BENEDICTION (PSALM 19)
   Let the words we speak this week be acceptable to you.
   May your Spirit be upon us.
   Let the thoughts of our minds be pleasing to you.
   May your Spirit be upon us.
   Let the meditations of our hearts be reflections of your
   heart.
   May your Spirit be upon us,
   sharing your Spirit with a world in need. Amen.

RESPONSIVE READING OR BENEDICTION
(LUKE 4)
   Christ has called us to bring good news to the poor.
   May the Spirit of God be upon us.

Christ sends us to proclaim release to the captives.
May the Spirit of God be upon us.
Christ calls us to bring sight to the blind.
May the Spirit of God be upon us.
Christ sends us to break the bonds of the oppressed.
May the Spirit of God be upon us.
Christ walks with us on this journey of ministry.
May the Spirit of God be upon us. Amen.

FEBRUARY 1, 2004

Fourth Sunday After the Epiphany
Brian Wren

COLOR
Green

SCRIPTURE READINGS
Jeremiah 1:4-10; Psalm 71:1-6; 1 Corinthians 13:1-13; Luke 4:21-30

THEME IDEAS
Jeremiah is appointed to speak for God to nations and kingdoms, but the power of his words will not protect him from abuse and contempt (see Jeremiah 11:18-23, 37:11–38:13). The psalmist, like Jeremiah, prays for deliverance from the unjust and the cruel. Jesus reminds his people about God's love for those beyond the bounds of patriotic pride, and is mobbed for it; later, he will be crucified for his words, as much as for his deeds. Paul unfolds a love that is gritty, detailed, and determined. The key question is: "Which scripture is most challenging and liberating to our congregation's particular context—and within the congregation, to women and men, elders and youth?"

CALL TO WORSHIP AND OPENING PRAYER (JEREMIAH 1, PSALM 71)
Here and now, we are in the presence of God,
who calls us from birth,

and knew us before we were born.
Living God, touch us with your love.
God knows us, but never intrudes.
God calls, but never compels.
God speaks, and waits for us to listen.
Living God, call us now.
Speak, that we may listen,
and together do your will,
through Jesus Christ. Amen.

CALL TO WORSHIP (JEREMIAH 1, 1 CORINTHIANS 13, LUKE 4)

Let us worship God.
Come, prepared to listen,
and then to speak to God.
Come, as the body of Christ,
learning how to practice
patience, honesty, and kindness.
Come, and follow Christ
beyond our tight frontiers of nation, race, and class.
Come, prepared to listen,
and then to live for God. Amen.

CONTEMPORARY GATHERING WORDS

Voice 1   So, what have you got for us today?
Voice 2   Words, and pictures in words.
Voice 1   Is that all? Will it be enough? Say more!
Jesus, saying how God loves foreigners;
a crowd, trying to throw him over a cliff;
Paul, saying how hard it is to love, and
how wonderful;
and a boy named Jeremiah, hearing
God's call.
Voice 2   He was only a boy?
Does God call children? Youth?
When they speak for God, do we listen?

Voice 1	Small words—and big questions.
Voice 2	Will they be enough?
Voice 1	We'll soon find out.
Voices 1 & 2	Let us worship God!

PRAISE SENTENCES (JEREMIAH 1, PSALM 71)

Let us praise God.
Before we were born, you knew us.
You took us from our mother's womb
and spoke our name with love. In Christ you love us
endlessly.
Therefore, in trouble and in joy,
always, we praise you.

OPENING PRAYER

Living God,
as you gather us in Christ, reveal among us now
the excellence of your love,
the evidence of our captivities,
and the invigoration of your Spirit.
Save us and inspire us
to be Christ's living body,
filled with faith, hope, and love.
In the name of Christ we pray.
Amen.

A LITANY OF CONFESSION AND LAMENT

[A stand alone Prayer, which can also be offered after, and in response to, Psalm 71 (Section 1), 1 Corinthians 13 (Section 2), and Luke 4 (Section 3), with echoes of Jeremiah 1:9.]

Let us come to Jesus Christ,
confessing our sin and our need.
Jesus our Savior, we praise you
that by the words of scripture
we are convicted, pardoned, and set free.

Risen Christ, alive among us,
save us and help us.

(1) If we benefit, day by day,
from institutions and arrangements
that hand out wounding words and cruel deeds,
Risen Christ, alive among us,
save us and help us.
If we endure, at the hand of others,
cruelty, injustice, and shame,
Risen Christ, alive among us,
save us and help us.

(2) If we have practiced selective compassion,
partial forgiveness,
part-time patience,
and limited kindness,
Risen Christ, alive among us,
save us and help us.

(3) If we have cheered God's love
for our nation, class, or race,
but recoiled from God's merciful kindness
to the other, the stranger, and the enemy,
Risen Christ, alive among us,
save us and help us.

Risen Christ, raise us to new life,
new hope, and new behavior.
We ask it in your name.
Amen.

BENEDICTION (JEREMIAH 1)
Do not say, "I am too young," "I am too old,"
"I am unqualified," "I am unworthy,"
"I am only this," or "I am only that,"

for the Living God declares,
"You shall go to whom I send you, and speak whatever I
command you.
Do not be afraid, for I am with you to deliver you."
Go then, as ambassadors, witnesses, and servants,
in the name of Jesus Christ,
and in the power of the Holy Spirit. Amen.

BENEDICTION (1 CORINTHIANS 13, REVISED ENGLISH BIBLE)

Go, as the body of Jesus Christ,
knowing there is nothing love cannot face,
no limit to its faith, its hope, and its endurance.
Go in peace. Amen.

© Copyright 2002 by Brian Wren

FEBRUARY 8, 2004

Fifth Sunday After the Epiphany
Sara Lambert

COLOR
Green

SCRIPTURE READINGS
Isaiah 6:1-8 (9-13); Psalm 138; 1 Corinthians 15:1-11; Luke 5:1-11

THEME IDEAS
As we sail with Christ upon the waters of life, we experience in these passages the steadfast love of the Lord who gives us strength and hope at all times. God's grace cleanses and saves us, and gives us hope for the future. We are encouraged to praise God's faithfulness, accept God's forgiveness, listen to God's word, and tell others the good news of Christ. The steps we must follow are also echoed in the words of Isaiah 6. More than a blueprint for worship, Isaiah helps us chart our spiritual journey: entering into discipleship, praising God, making confession, asking for forgiveness, and hearing and responding to God's word.

CALL TO WORSHIP (ISAIAH 6)
Holy, holy, holy is the Lord of hosts.
God, the whole earth is full of your glory!
We come to praise and exalt the name of the Lord.
O God, the whole earth is full of your glory!

Let us put aside our cares to worship the Lord.
O God, the whole earth is full of your glory!
Glory to God in the highest!
O God, the whole earth is full of your glory!

CALL TO WORSHIP (LUKE 5)

We are gathered at the lakeshore to hear the word of God.
Carry us in your boat, O Lord, and teach us.
We are prepared to cast our nets in faith and love.
We yearn to be amazed at our catch and follow Christ today.
As we worship together, may we feel the breath of God blowing us toward clear skies and bountiful seas.
Praise God whose wisdom and grace guide our way.

CONTEMPORARY GATHERING WORDS (ISAIAH 6, 1 CORINTHIANS 15, LUKE 5)

God welcomes us with open arms!
We come to worship you, God!
Jesus will teach us amazing things!
We come to praise you, Jesus!
The Holy Spirit will guide our hearts!
We come to listen to you, Spirit.
With God's grace, we begin this time together in hope and joy!

PRAISE SENTENCES (PSALM 138)

Praise God for steadfast love and faithfulness that endure forever! Whenever we ask, the Lord gives us strength for our souls. In times of trouble, the hand of God stretches out to save us.

PRAISE SENTENCES (ISAIAH 6)

Holy, holy, holy is the Lord of hosts!
Praise God who calls us to go out in the world with joy!

PRAISE SENTENCES (LUKE 5)

Christ teaches us to "catch people" with love! Like the
first disciples, faith will fill our nets with the amazing
love of Christ!

OPENING PRAYER (LUKE 5)

Lord of hope and strength,
  be with us this day as we strive to follow you.
May our faith be as deep as the sea—
  deep enough to carry us to peaceful shores.
Nurture us in your love,
  and guide us with your grace.
In Christ's name we pray. Amen.

OPENING PRAYER (ISAIAH 6, PSALM 138)

God of the ages,
  we give thanks for your steadfast love and faithfulness.
We come to you today with open hearts and open minds,
  ready to praise your name.
May our journey together be fruitful
  as we continue to seek your purpose for us.
Amen.

PRAYER OF CONFESSION (PSALM 138, ISAIAH 6, LUKE 5, 1 CORINTHIANS)

Holy One, we know that your grace is given to us freely
  yet we find it difficult to grasp your acceptance.
We have been unclean in many ways,
  yet you cleanse us.
We experience the rolling seas of life
  with the disappointment of failure,
  yet you stretch out your calming hand of strength
  to comfort and guide us.
You sent us your only Son that we might be saved,
  yet we continue to falter.
Lord, we ask for your love and grace once again,

that you might make us whole to follow Christ,
who teaches us your forgiveness.
Amen.

BENEDICTION (PSALM 138, ISAIAH 6, LUKE 5, 1 CORINTHIANS 15)

May the God of hope and strength go with us today.
We feel your love, O Lord.
May the amazing grace of Christ inspire our journeys.
We know your grace, O Lord.
We hear the voice of the Lord saying, "Whom shall I send?"
We hear your voice, O Lord.
We long to say with Isaiah, "Here am I; send me!"

FEBRUARY 15, 2004

Sixth Sunday After the Epiphany

Linda Lee

COLOR

Green

SCRIPTURE READINGS

Jeremiah 17:5-10; Psalm 1; 1 Corinthians 15:12-20; Luke 6:17-26

THEME IDEAS

Today's focus includes the benefits of trusting God, and the loss incurred when we turn away from God. The scriptures describe both the blessings of God's kingdom, and the consequences of putting earthly rewards above the benefits God offers. Christians embrace these blessings and benefits with confidence, because they are grounded in Christ's resurrection from the dead. Today is also the day after Valentine's Day and the midpoint of Black History Month. In both cases, the theme of trust is central. Trust in God is both an historical legacy and a present necessity, if loving relationships between people, and faith and hope, are to overcome trial and adversity.

CALL TO WORSHIP (JEREMIAH 17)

Blessed are those who trust in the Lord,
whose trust is the Lord.

**They shall be like a tree planted by water,
sending out its roots by the stream.**
They shall not fear the heat,
nor wither in the sun.
**In the year of drought they are not anxious,
for their lives do not cease to bear fruit.**
Come all you who trust in the Lord!
Let us worship!

CALL TO WORSHIP (PSALM 1)

You, who delight in the law of the Lord,
and who meditate on God's law, day and night,
are like trees planted by streams of water.
**God's word is a lamp unto our feet,
and a light unto our path.**
The watery grave of your ancestors
yields fruit in due season,
when justice has prevailed.
Our leaves do not wither. Christ is risen!

CALL TO WORSHIP (LUKE 6)

Blessed are you who hunger. Come and be filled.
We come, hungering for justice and righteousness.
Blessed are you who weep. Come and be comforted.
We come, seeking joy and laughter.
Blessed are you who suffer for Christ. Come and be
Christ's chosen ones.
We come, yearning for strength to persevere.
Come, the worship of God is our joy and our strength.

CONTEMPORARY GATHERING WORDS (JEREMIAH 17)

We come, like trees in need of strong roots.
We will live in God's love.
We come, like plants in need of a drink.
We will drink of Christ's mercy.

We come, like fruit in need of bright sunshine.
We will soak up the Spirit's strength.

PRAISE SENTENCES (1 CORINTHIANS 15)

We proclaim Christ crucified and risen from the dead.
Christ is risen!
Is Christ risen?
Christ is risen! Christ is risen indeed!

OPENING PRAYER (1 CORINTHIANS 15)

O God, our help in ages past, our hope for years to come, during this month in which the contributions of the daughters and sons of Africa are honored and remembered, let us honor and celebrate their trust in you. Their trust in the resurrection of Jesus Christ has resurrected their hope, their courage, and their love, again and again. Give us that same trust in these perilous days, that our hope in you might be secure. Amen.

PRAYER OF CONFESSION (LUKE 6)

Dear God,
    bless us during this month of hope remembered,
    and dreams no longer deferred.
We confess our poverty of spirit,
    our spiritual hunger, and our grief.
Have mercy on us for our hatred,
    our exclusion of others, and our disrespect for the
    people who have suffered at our expense.
Heal us of the sin and shame of racism and prejudice.
Show us how to love others as you have loved us.
Amen.

BENEDICTION

We go from this place as those who are blessed!
We are filled.

We have joy.
We have all we need.
From this place we go to give, to bear fruit, to love.
Our trust, O God, is in you!

FEBRUARY 22, 2004

Seventh Sunday After the Epiphany/Transfiguration Sunday
Roger Dowdy

COLOR
White or Gold

SCRIPTURE READINGS
Exodus 34:29-35; Psalm 99; 2 Corinthians 3:12–4:2; Luke 9:28-36 (37-43*a*)

THEME IDEAS
Literally meaning "to go beyond appearance," the transfiguration of Jesus contains images of brilliance, power, and the glory of God—all in the context of fervent, listening prayer (Luke 9:28). Experiencing the raw power of the glory of God, when revealed in the transfigured Christ, overwhelmed the disciples. Rather than be present to the radical experience of God's glory, Peter avoids it by seeking to construct booths—memorial symbols of the Israelite's Exodus from Egypt (compare the festival of *Sukkoth*). This service would be a powerful context for Holy Communion, inviting the congregation to experience the mystery, glory, and call of the presence of Christ in the Eucharist. The Transfiguration is pivotal in the worship lectionary readings because it appears on the

Sunday before Lent, when we participate in Jesus' journey to Jerusalem.

OPENING WORDS

We come into this holy place, invited by Christ. As Peter, James, and John came to the mountaintop with Christ, we come to witness, in awe and wonder, God moving and speaking in our midst. May our minds, our very heart and soul, be awakened to the awesome power of God at work. And through God's mighty power and glory, may we be shaped in the image of Christ in this time of worship. So may it be! Thanks be to God.

CALL TO WORSHIP

Holy is the Lord!
Let us praise God's great and wondrous name!
The Lord's brightness shines upon us.
We will pray and sing in glad thanksgiving to God.
The Lord hears and answers the songs and prayers of the faithful.
We will call on God in fervent prayer and praise!
Holy is the Lord!
Alleluia!

PRAISE SENTENCES (PSALM 99)

Christ is exalted. God is exalted. Christ is exalted on high!

OPENING PRAYER

God of earth and sky, God of all times and places, we have come to this place to be your people. You have called to us, and we feel a deep longing to know you, to hear you speak to us, to be your church. Just as you revealed your glory to the prophet Moses, as he stood on the mountaintop to receive the Ten Commandments, your glory was seen anew when Jesus stood transfigured before his disciples on the mountaintop. May we not be blinded by your light, but be strengthened by it. With your help, may we see and hear what you have to say to us. Through the power of your Holy Spirit, and by the presence of Christ with us, open our eyes and ears and hearts to know the brightness of your glory. Amen.

PRAYER OF CONFESSION

Holy God, our creator and giver of life, we are humbled by your love and power. Because of your great love for us, we come to you with our individual and collective prayers of confession—confession of things we have done that have hurt or caused pain to others and to ourselves, confession of things we have done that have kept us from being who you intend us to be. *(silence)* We confess our failure to remember your Word, made known to us through Christ, and confess that we have forgotten the Word that you speak to us through the calls, of friends, through unspoken signs from coworkers, through the love of family, through the cries of need in our community. *(silence)* Break open our hardened hearts, unstop our ears, open our eyes, that we might come to know the peace and freedom that are gifts from living in the glory of your love and grace. Transfigure us into the kind of persons that reflect your brightness—a brightness that reveals justice, kindness, compassion, and mercy. *(silence)* We pray this in the holy name of your Son, the Chosen One, Jesus Christ. Amen.

RESPONSE TO THE WORD

What have you heard?
We have heard the proclamation of a wondrous and mysterious story—a story of Christ's call to his disciples to witness, to experience the glory of God.

What have you heard?

We have heard God speak to the disciples on the mountaintop, calling them to see and to listen.

How will you act on what you have heard?

We will seek to let the mind of Christ dwell in us with our whole being. With God's help, we will strive to let the Spirit that dwells in us shine—shine brightly in our homes and neighborhoods, workplace and community—shine brightly that God's will be done and God's kingdom come.

Let us affirm what we believe:

[Select one of several Affirmations of Faith—see especially The United Methodist Hymnal: *888, 889, or others.]*

BENEDICTION

May the transfiguring love of God be known in the world—known by the way we live and speak and serve.

Amen.

May the transfiguring grace of Jesus Christ be shown in us—shown by where and how we live and work.

Amen.

May the transfiguring power of God's Holy Spirit guide— guide us in ways of justice, mercy, and kindness.

Amen.

The peace of the Lord be with you always.

And also with you.

BENEDICTION

God calls us, just as God called the three disciples on the mountaintop, to listen to God's Chosen One, Jesus.

With God's help, we will open our minds and hearts and ears to Christ.

Christ calls us to behold the glory of God's kingdom, made known in prayer.

May we, in our praying, be filled with the brightness of God's glory, that through us, God's glory may become real to those in need.

God's transforming love go with you.
And with you also.
The richness of the grace of Jesus Christ abide in you.
And also in you.
The renewing power of the Holy Spirit sustain you in your daily service.
And you also. Amen.

FEBRUARY 25, 2004

Ash Wednesday

B. J. Beu

COLOR

Purple or Gray

SCRIPTURE READINGS

Joel 2:1-2, 12-17; Psalm 51:1-17; 2 Corinthians 5:20b–6:10;
Matthew 6:1-6, 16-21

THEME IDEAS

Ash Wednesday begins the great journey of Lent—the
journey of turning away from sinful pursuits, the journey
of preparing to follow Christ's steps to Jerusalem, the
journey of turning toward the cross. Ash Wednesday
begins a period of somber introspection. We are not the
center of the universe; we are not even the center of our
own existence. Christ is. Through the imposition of ashes
on our foreheads, we are reminded of the frailty of our
lives here on earth, for we were created out of the dust,
and to dust we shall return. While a dominant theme of
Ash Wednesday is contrition for past transgressions, that
is by no means the only theme. Divine judgment is at
hand, but that judgment is imbued with mercy. For
Christ did not come to condemn the world, but to save it.
God does not desire that we rend our clothes for our sins,
but that we rend our hearts. Ash Wednesday presents the
promise and hope of salvation when we return to God.

CALL TO WORSHIP (JOEL 2)

Blow the trumpet in Zion.
Sound the alarm on God's holy mountain!
The day of the Lord draws near—
a day of darkness and gloom.
Yet even now, God is calling us
to turn from our transgressions.
We will return to God with all our hearts!
God does not desire us to rend our clothing.
We will rend our hearts instead.
Our God is gracious and merciful
Our God abounds in steadfast love!

CALL TO WORSHIP (PSALM 51)

Have mercy on us, O God.
Bathe us in your steadfast love.
Wash us thoroughly from our iniquities.
Cleanse us from our sin.
Create in us a clean heart, O God.
We will sing aloud our deliverance!
Open our lips, O God.
We will sing aloud your praise!

CONTEMPORARY GATHERING WORDS (JOEL 2)

Return to the Lord, judgment is drawing near.
We will return to the Lord.
Return to the Lord, for God is gracious and merciful.
We will return to the Lord.
Return to the Lord with all your heart.
We will return to the Lord.

CONTEMPORARY GATHERING WORDS (PSALM 51)

We come to the fount of Living Water.
Wash away our sin!
We come seeking the truth of your salvation.
Grant us wisdom!

We come to be made whole.
Put your Spirit within us!

PRAISE SENTENCES (2 CORINTHIANS 5)

Christ came to reconcile us with God.
Christ be praised!
Christ came for our salvation.
Christ be praised!
Christ came to make us holy.
Christ be praised!

OPENING PRAYER (JOEL 2)

Creator God,
> you fashioned us from the dust of the earth,
> and to dust we shall return.
Help us to hear the trumpet in Zion,
> heralding that the day of the Lord draws near.
Draw us back to you, O God,
> for you are gracious and merciful,
> slow to anger and abounding in steadfast love.
Heal the hardness of our hearts,
> that we may be faithful disciples of the One
> who was nailed to a cross for our transgressions.
Amen.

OPENING PRAYER

God of earth and water, God of dust and ash,
> you are all around us, nearer than our own breath.
May the ashes placed upon our foreheads this day
> remind us of who we are, and whose we are.
May these ashes remind us of the frailty of our lives
> and of our need to live each day to the fullest.
May these ashes be a sign of our willingness to face our
> mistakes—a promise to commit ourselves to leading
> more godly lives.

We pray this in the name of the One who makes all things
new. Amen.

PRAYER OF CONFESSION (MATTHEW 6)

Gracious God,
> too often we have sought recognition for our piety.

We have taken pride in our giving, congratulated ourselves for caring about our neighbors,
> and sought to be recognized for our devotion to you.

Correct our wayward feet.

And make us fit to inherit your kingdom,
> through Jesus Christ our Lord. Amen.

BENEDICTION

God made us from the dust to give us life.
> **We cherish God's gift.**

Christ saved us from the cross to give us life.
> **We cherish Christ's gift.**

Go with God's blessing.

FEBRUARY 29, 2004

First Sunday in Lent
Kirsi Stjerna

COLOR
Purple or Blue

SCRIPTURE READINGS
Deuteronomy 26:1-11; Psalm 91:1-2, 9-16; Romans 10:8*b*-13; Luke 4:1-13

THEME IDEAS
God is our refuge, our consoling embrace, our nourishing sustenance. As parents and as children, we need affirmation of the intentions and care of our heavenly parent. In God's way of relating to us, we learn how to provide for the refuge, embrace, and sustenance of our own children; and we learn how to enjoy the refuge, embrace, and sustenance of our parents. We seek for understanding and compassion when the care we give or enjoy falters. With our faults, fears, and failures, we can expect to find refuge and perspective from our Divine Parent, whose ways are beyond all hurt. And yet pain and misfortune happen. In the midst of our hurt, rather than "tempting" ourselves and God with false expectations of pain-free lives for ourselves and our children, we can trust that God is there when we fall, shielding the blow so that we don't break ourselves against the stones of life's misfortunes.

CALL TO WORSHIP OR GATHERING WORDS (ROMANS 10)

We come together in the presence of our heavenly parent:
to confess, to proclaim, to hear God's promise, to share our burdens, and to sing our song of joy.

GATHERING WORDS (ROMANS 10, PSALM 91)

As mothers and fathers, daughters and sons,
we come together.
The Word is near.
We come to share, to affirm, to rejoice.
God is our refuge and our dwelling place.
We seek comfort, guidance, wisdom, and care.
God, in you we trust.

CONTEMPORARY GATHERING WORDS (ROMANS 10, PSALM 91)

The word is near you, on your lips and in your heart.
Praise God!
Those who call on the name of God will be heard.
Praise God!
Those who look for shelter in God will find it.
Praise God!
Let us rejoice and sing.

PRAISE SENTENCES (PSALM 91, ROMANS 10)

I praise my God, my refuge and my safety.
I sing to my God whom I trust.
The Word is near.
God is near.

UNISON PRAYER (PSALM 91)

God, you have promised to deliver those who love you. You have promised to protect those who know your name. Trusting in your promise, we ask you to rescue us, and bless us with fullness of life and eternal peace. In the name of the One who is our heavenly mother and father, we pray. Amen.

BENEDICTION (PSALM 91)

May the God who loves us like a mother and a father,
    guard us and protect our children from all harm.
May the God who protects us like a mother and a father,
    shield us and our children from all evil.
May the One who loves us fiercely, keep us,
    that we may not dash our foot against a stone,
    but will live to behold our salvation.

BENEDICTION

Let us go in peace and confidence, remembering . . .
    God is our refuge.
Let us rejoice and be consoled with the assurance . . .
    God is our salvation.
Thanks be to God,
    our refuge and our salvation.

MARCH 7, 2004

Second Sunday in Lent
Mary J. Scifres

COLOR
Purple or Blue

SCRIPTURE READINGS
Genesis 15:1-12, 17-18; Psalm 27; Philippians 3:17–4:1; Luke 13:31-35

THEME IDEAS
Trusting in God's promises is not an easy task. Even so, God asks us to do that time and again—from the time of Abraham facing his wife's barrenness, to the time of the early church wondering when Christ would return. The words of the psalmist remind us that we need not fear, for God is always with us. During this Lenten season, waiting and trusting are themes that help us to prepare for Holy Week.

CALL TO WORSHIP (PSALM 27)
Christ is my light and my salvation.
   I shall not be afraid!
God is the strength of my life.
   I shall not be afraid!
One thing I ask of God:
   to live in God's house all the days of my life, and to see God's face and worship in God's holy presence.

Let us come into God's presence to seek Christ's light.
Let us worship God together.

CALL TO WORSHIP (PSALM 27)

Wait for the Lord.
We come, waiting for the wisdom of God to guide us.
Wait for the Lord.
We come, waiting for the grace of Christ Jesus to flow over us.
Wait for the Lord.
We come, waiting for the strength of the Holy Spirit to fill us.
Wait for the Lord.
Come to us, Holy One, full of wisdom, grace, and strength. Amen.

CONTEMPORARY GATHERING WORDS (LUKE 13)

Blessed is the one who comes in the name of the Lord!
Blessed be the Lord God of Israel!
Blessed is the one who comes in the name of the Lord!
Blessed be the Lord God of Israel!
Blessed is the one who comes in the name of the Lord!
Blessed be the Lord God of Israel!

CONTEMPORARY GATHERING WORDS (PSALM 27)

The Lord is my light and my salvation.
Whom shall I fear?
I fear nothing, for God is with me!
The Lord is my light and my salvation.
Whom shall I fear?
I fear nothing, for God is with me!
The Lord is my light and my salvation.
Whom shall I fear?
I fear nothing, for God is with me!

PRAISE SENTENCES (PSALM 27)

Let's sing and make music to the Lord!
Let's sing and make music to the Lord!

OPENING PRAYER (PSALM 27, PHILIPPIANS 3)

O God, our Rock and our Redeemer,
    hide us in your shelter this day.
As we come into your presence with songs and prayers,
    let our time of worship bring us closer to you.
Lift up our hearts,
    that we might seek you and know your ways.
Set our minds on your thoughts,
    that we might live as your people.
In the name of Christ, our Light and our Life, we pray.
Amen.

OPENING PRAYER (PHILIPPIANS 3)

God of hope and salvation,
    help us to set our minds on heavenly things
    during this time of worship.
Infuse us with your grace and your guidance
    that when we leave this place,
    we might bring a bit of heaven into your world. Amen.

OPENING PRAYER (LUKE 13)

Gather us in, Christ Jesus.
Be as a mother to us when we scatter and stray,
    and call us home into your community of faith.
Help us to hear your call, and to seek your voice, in
    all that we do and all that we say. Amen.

PRAYER OF CONFESSION (PSALM 27, PHILIPPIANS 3)

God of grace and power,
    we confess that we often do not trust you with our
    lives.

We are too easily betrayed by our doubts,
even when signs of your promise are all around us.
Forgive us our doubts.
Help our doubts to blossom into flowers of faith and
hope, that we might become a people of firm convic-
tion and strong courage.
Let your strength grow in us,
that we might say with the songwriter,
"The Lord is my light and my salvation!
Of whom shall I be afraid?"

Words of Assurance

The Lord is our light and our saving grace! Nothing can
separate us from the light and love of God made known
in Christ Jesus. Put aside fear, and trust in God, for we
have nothing to fear!

Prayer (Psalm 27)

God, be a shield of grace and strength in our lives.
Help us to find the path of faith,
even when we doubt your promises.
Light our way in the darkness,
and show us the road to salvation.
During these weeks of Lent,
let each step we take draw us closer to you,
as we seek your presence in our lives. Amen.

Benediction (Philippians 3)

Take courage my friends, and go forth as God's people!

Benediction (Philippians 3)

Stand firm in the Lord.
Be strong and courageous.
Trust in God's promises.
And walk in God's ways. Amen.

MARCH 14, 2004

Third Sunday in Lent
Nancy Crawford Holm

COLOR
Purple or Blue

SCRIPTURE READINGS
Isaiah 55:1-9; Psalm 63:1-8; 1 Corinthians 10:1-13; Luke 13:1-9

THEME IDEAS
Preparation for the honoring and celebration of the death and resurrection of Christ continues through this third Sunday in Lent. Focusing on simplicity, emptiness, and repentance is appropriate. Themes specific to the lections are: thirst, mercy, standing firm in the test of faith, and turning from sin. Consider also the theme of desert (or its equivalent in your geographical location), and the themes of barrenness and God's expectations for us as seen in Jesus' parable of the fig tree.

CALL TO WORSHIP (ISAIAH 55)
Let all who thirst come to the water.
We come, seeking God's living water!
Let all who hunger come join the feast.
We come, seeking God's heavenly food—
food that satisfies our deepest desires!
Let all who mourn come and be comforted.

We come, seeking fellowship with our living and loving God. We join our voices, our hearts, and our lives, on this journey to be people of God made whole.

CALL TO WORSHIP

Come worship the Lord!
We come burdened with sorrow.
God welcomes all seekers.
We come with concerns.
Come worship together the God who loves us and whose door is always open to us.
We come in anticipation of the miraculous moving of God's spirit. Come, let us worship the Lord!

CALL TO WORSHIP (LUKE 13)

Faith is the gift of God. Come worship our Creator and feed your faith.
God is like a gardener who won't let beloved plants wither.
Faith is the gift of God. Lift praise to Jesus Christ and find the way to new life.
Jesus is like a gardener who tends and fertilizes the soil of our hearts.
Faith is the gift of God. Call upon the Holy Spirit and grow in discipleship.
The Holy Spirit is like a gardener coaxing us to bear fruit that will glorify God. (Sherry Parker)

PRAISE SENTENCES (PSALM 63)

God, our wonderful God, we see your power and glory. Praise to you, our God, whose constant love is better than life. We lift your name above all names. We bless you all the days of our lives!

OPENING PRAYER

God of the ages, of the barren desert, and of infinite love, guide us in our seeking.

Lead us in our searching.
Open our eyes to our failings,
    that we might turn to you and be renewed. Amen.

PRAYER OF CONFESSION

As much as we desire to love and serve you, God,
    we do not always do what we know is right.
We say what we wish we had not said,
    and we savor thoughts that we later regret.
For all that should not have been, we ask your
    forgiveness.
Please renew our desire and give us strength to begin
    again. Amen.

BENEDICTION (LUKE 13)

Go forth bearing fruit.
For the God of infinite patience
    has graced you with forgiveness,
    and walks with you each step of the way.
Carry on, redeemed people of the God of Love!

MARCH 21, 2004

Fourth Sunday in Lent/One Great Hour of Sharing

B. J. Beu

COLOR

Purple or Blue

SCRIPTURE READINGS

Joshua 5:9-12; Psalm 32; 2 Corinthians 5:16-21; Luke 15:1-3, 11*b*-32

THEME IDEAS

When the youngest son returns home in the parable of the prodigal son, the father says to his servant: "Get the fatted calf and kill it, and let us eat and celebrate; for this son of mine was dead and is alive again; he was lost and is found!" Herein lies a central insight of the gospel, indeed of all scripture. There is something worse than death, and that is to be lost. And there is something better than life, and that is to be found. The prophets came, that we might be reconciled to God. Christ came to reconcile the world to God. When we follow God faithfully, as Joshua did, we eat from the fat of the land. When we follow Christ faithfully, we are a new creation, for we were lost, but now are found.

CALL TO WORSHIP (PSALM 32)

Be glad in the Lord and rejoice.
We rejoice in the Lord!

Shout for joy, all you upright in heart.
We shout for joy in the Lord!
For God has forgiven our transgressions.
God has set our hearts free!
Be glad in the Lord and rejoice.
We rejoice in the Lord!

CALL TO WORSHIP (LUKE 15)

Like a loving Father,
you offer us freedom to choose our own path.
We worship you, O God!
Like a merciful Father,
you are filled with compassion when we lose our way.
We worship you, O God!
Like a forgiving Father,
you receive us back into your arms.
We worship you, O God!

CONTEMPORARY GATHERING WORDS (2 CORINTHIANS 5)

Christ came to make the world new again.
We come to be made new!
Christ came to make the world whole again.
We come to be made whole!
Christ came to offer the world God's love.
We come to offer our love back to God.

CONTEMPORARY GATHERING WORDS (JOSHUA 5, LUKE 15)

The Lord has rolled away our disgrace.
We were lost, but now are found!
The Lord has fed us with heavenly food!
In Christ, we are fed!
The Lord rejoices in our salvation!
We rejoice in the Lord!

PRAISE SENTENCES (2 CORINTHIANS 5)

Christ has reconciled the world to himself.
Praise be to God!
Christ has made all things new.
Praise be to God!
In Christ we are a new creation.
Praise be to God!

PRAISE SENTENCES (PSALM 32)

Be glad in the Lord and rejoice.
We rejoice in the Lord!
Shout for joy, you upright in heart.
We shout for joy in our God!
Sing to the Lord a new song.
We sing praises to the Lord, our God!

OPENING PRAYER (ONE GREAT HOUR OF SHARING)

God of overflowing abundance,
    you bless the earth and it brings forth food.
May we, who have been given so much,
    think of those who are in want.
May we, who enjoy the bounty of this good land,
    think of those whose lands are plagued by famine,
    pestilence, and war.
May we, who call ourselves Christ's disciples,
    give freely of our worldly riches,
    just as Christ gave freely of the heavenly kingdom.
Amen.

OPENING PRAYER OR PRAYER OF CONFESSION AND ASSURANCE (LUKE 15)

Merciful God, you seek not to punish the sinner,
    but to restore the lost to righteousness.
When we are dead to our sins, restore us to life.

When we go astray, receive us back into your arms,
 as the prodigal son was welcomed home by his father.
For your steadfast love knows no bounds,
 your loving embrace is always there for us.
In your love, O God, we are never lost.
In your care, we are ever found.
Help us find our way home,
 that we may taste the heavenly banquet
 prepared for your beloved children.
In Jesus' name we pray. Amen.

PRAYER OF CONFESSION AND ASSURANCE (PSALM 32)

O God, you are our hiding place, our shelter from trouble. When we come to you and confess our transgressions, you forgive us the guilt of our sin. Why then do we tarry? Why do we delay coming before you with pleading hearts? Hear our prayer, O God. Heed the confession of our lips, that we may be numbered among the happy ones whose transgressions are forgiven. We rejoice that you hear us and deliver us from all evil, through the One who bore our transgressions. Amen.

BENEDICTION (2 CORINTHIANS 5)

In Christ, we are a new creation.
In Christ, we are made anew!
In Christ, we are reconciled with God.
In Christ, we are made anew!
In Christ, we are ambassadors of the Living God.
In Christ, we are made anew!

MARCH 28, 2004

Fifth Sunday in Lent
Christine Boardman

COLOR
Purple or Blue

SCRIPTURE READINGS
Isaiah 43:16-21; Psalm 126; Philippians 3:4b-14; John 12:1-8

THEME IDEAS
The fifth Sunday of Lent brings us closer to Holy Week, a time of lament. We press on to Easter, a time of hope. As we journey, let's explore the theme of extravagant, unconditional love. The Holy One of creation promises and provides all that we need. We are loved over and over again, from our sorrowing, weeping past, into a fruitful and new future. The ethic of love, shown in extravagant ways, claims us, and we acknowledge the many opportunities to serve others in this world of hope and lament, in this world of extravagant, unconditional love.

CALL TO WORSHIP (ISAIAH 43)
Come, chosen people of faith, to receive God's provisions!
We come, awaiting God's goodness.
Come, chosen people of faith, to seek solace for our sorrow!

We come, formed by God's refreshing and unconditional love.
Come, chosen people of faith, to declare praise to our God!
We come, to worship the God who is doing a new thing in this world.

CALL TO WORSHIP (JOHN 12)

Let us gather as Jesus' disciples and be in his presence. Here in this holy place, let us breathe in the power of God's promise of strength for the journey of faith, and release all that would hinder us from showing our love for this world. Like Mary of Bethany, may we find and offer something costly of ourselves, to serve others. And like Jesus, awaken us to the promise of new life for the world, this community, and for each one. Amen.

[This call is very effective with two liturgical dancers or clowns entering the sanctuary and walking to the chancel. Then, sit at the foot of a cross, if possible. Facing one another, rise, gather in air and push away air with your arms demonstrating the collective breath. Try to use large props: a jar of liquid and a plant for new life. Be sure to broadly smile as you leave the chancel, waving at the community of faith.]

UNISON PRAYER (JOHN 12)

O God of extravagant love, touch us where we are road-weary and where we are the most fearful. Open our lives to the living word that restores our hope, giving us meaning and purpose. Help us to leave behind all that hinders us from following Christ to the cross, and beyond.

CONTEMPORARY GATHERING WORDS (PHILIPPIANS 3)

Press on, press on . . . the goal is love.
God is love.

Press on, press on . . . the goal is life.
Christ is life.
Press on, press on . . . the goal is love.
God is love.
Press on, press on . . . the goal is life.
Christ is life.

OPENING PRAYER

Hear us, O God, as we gather to sing your praise,
to recount our story of faith,
and to be refreshed for the journey that awaits us.
Help us awaken to the opportunities all around us—
opportunities to demonstrate a love that is both costly
and extravagant.
Anoint us, as we gather together.
Help us look beyond our past,
and welcome the new life that you alone make possible.
Amen.

PRAYER OF CONFESSION (PHILIPPIANS 3)

O God, we have been slow to leave our past behind, and
move forward in faith. There are so many roadblocks that
you alone can remove. There are faults in others that we are
slow to forget and forgive. There are times when we dwell
on things that we cannot change. We have chosen perfec-
tionism and self-righteousness. Forgive us, O God. Help us
offer our faith in Christ to others, without so many roadblocks. Strengthen our resolve, as we run this race of faith.
Free us to love, O God. Keep us within your care, that we
may be guided to follow Christ where he leads us. Save us
from the sin that holds us back, and grant that we may hear
your call to move ahead with a sense of mission. Forgive
us, free us, and save us as people of the resurrection. Amen.

BENEDICTION

Go now into the world, full of the refreshment and
resilience God provides. You have been anointed. Keep

persevering in your faithful witness and service. Press on, press on, brothers and sisters in Christ. Remember, there is no desert or wilderness, no spiritual famine or warring madness, where God is not present. You are a blessed and a chosen people. Share your praise of God, as you move to new life in Christ. Go now to seek the play that nourishes, the good work that satisfies, and the relationships that offer extravagant and unconditional love. And let the people say, amen.

APRIL 4, 2004

Palm/Passion Sunday

Laura Jaquith Bartlett

COLOR
Purple or Blue

PALM SUNDAY READINGS
Psalm 118:1-2, 19-29; Luke 19:28-40

PASSION SUNDAY READINGS
Isaiah 50:4-9*a*; Psalm 31:9-16; Philippians 2:5-11; Luke 22:14–23:56 (or Luke 23:1-49)

THEME IDEAS
Even though this day bears dual identities as Palm and Passion Sunday, the scripture readings for both emphasize the everlasting quality of God's love. Perhaps, especially on this day as we move into Holy Week, we need that love more than ever. Most of us will start the morning shouting "Glory to the King!" only to discover that this "king" rides a borrowed colt, endures taunts, betrayal, and torture, and is finally killed as a common criminal. Some king! But this is when we must cling to the sure knowledge, as the Scriptures affirm, that God's love never deserted Jesus, and will never desert us. God's steadfast love endures forever!

CALL TO WORSHIP (PSALM 118)

O give thanks to the Lord, for God is good.
God's steadfast love endures forever!
This is the day that the Lord has made.
Let us rejoice and be glad in it!

CALL TO WORSHIP (PALM SUNDAY)

Blessed is the One who comes in the name of the Lord.
Glory in the highest heaven!
Blessed are you who proclaim the glory of God.
Hosanna in the highest!

CONTEMPORARY GATHERING WORDS (LUKE 19)

May I have your attention, please? We're about to begin.
Hey! The One who comes in God's name is the greatest!
Quiet down, please, and assume a worshipful attitude.
Jesus is coming, and we're going to shout our praise to the highest heaven!
I really must ask you to stop all this commotion in church.
If we stop shouting, the rocks will do it for us. Jesus is coming, and we're going to tell the world!

CONTEMPORARY GATHERING WORDS (PSALM 118)

Swing wide the city gates, the righteous gates!
We'll walk right through and praise God!
O God, you have truly become our salvation.
Let's celebrate and be festive!
O God, we lift high your praise.
Thank you, God. Your love never quits!

OPENING PRAYER (PALM SUNDAY)

O God, we look for you to come sweeping into the world
in a presidential motorcade, with sirens blaring and flags

flying. And meanwhile you have already come, trotting over the cobblestones on a borrowed colt, without fanfare, but with the voices of believers shouting out the good news: your love is everlasting! Be with us on this Palm Sunday, as we join our voices of praise with our sisters and brothers around the world. All glory to you, O God, your love is everlasting! Amen.

OPENING PRAYER (PASSION SUNDAY, PSALM 118)

When we are in trouble, God, we turn to you. Even in deep, deep trouble, you are the one who is still there. When our friends turn out to be fair-weather companions, when gossip gets out of control, when all we can do is cry—even then, you are there. Every hour of every day is in your hands. Our salvation is your never-ending love for us. Amen.

PRAYER OF CONFESSION

Forgiving God, we come to you shouting, "Hosanna!" Yet we are all too aware that we would rather stay on the street corner, joyfully watching the parade. We do not want to be a part of the betrayal, the trial, the crucifixion, the pain. Merciful God, we need you to lead us through the days ahead. Help us to know your presence in the hard times, even as we trust that you will guide us on to the victory of your resurrection. Amen.

BENEDICTION

As we leave this place, God's never-ending love goes with us.

As we journey through the days of Holy Week, God's never-ending love will guide us.

As we anticipate the joy of gathering again on Easter morning, God's never-ending love will be there, waiting for us.

Thanks be to God!

BENEDICTION

Go now, for we know that this is the day that the Lord has made.

God's love never quits!

Go now, for we proclaim that Jesus is ruler over all.

God's love never quits!

Go now, for we move with the Spirit, ready to face the days ahead.

God's love never quits! Hosanna in the highest!

APRIL 8, 2004

Holy Thursday

B. J. Beu

COLOR
Purple or Blue

SCRIPTURE READINGS
Exodus 12:1-4 (5-10) 11-14; Psalm 116:1-4, 12-19;
1 Corinthians 11:23-26; John 13:1-17, 31b-35

THEME IDEAS
Holy Thursday, also known as Maundy Thursday, recalls
Christ's celebration of the Passover feast with his disciples on the night before he was crucified. The Passover
feast itself recalls the mercy of God, when God passed
over the homes of the Hebrew people in Egypt, sparing
them from the death of every firstborn in the land. On
Holy Thursday, Christ re-images this traditional
Passover meal, replacing the meat and blood of the sacrificial lamb with his own body and blood, which
became the church's sacrament of Holy Communion.
John's account of Holy Thursday includes Christ washing the feet of his disciples. By washing their feet, Christ
shows that all are called to servant ministry; and Christ
leaves his disciples with a final commandment: to love
one another, for his disciples will be known for their love
of one another.

CALL TO WORSHIP (PSALM 116)

Snares of death surround us. Call on the name of the Lord and be saved.
The Lord is the cup of our salvation!
Pangs of suffering and grief enfold us.
Call on the name of the Lord and be saved.
The Lord is the cup of our salvation!
Bonds of distress and anguish bind us.
Call on the name of the Lord and be saved.
The Lord is the cup of our salvation!

CALL TO WORSHIP OR INVITATION TO COMMUNION (1 CORINTHIANS 11)

Christ's body was broken for us, that we might be made one and whole.
We are made one and whole in Christ's body, broken for us.
Christ's blood was poured out for us, that our sins might be forgiven.
We are forgiven through Christ's blood, shed for us.
The Lord's Supper is a foretaste of the heavenly banquet prepared for us by Christ.
Taste and see that the Lord is good.

CONTEMPORARY GATHERING WORDS (JOHN 13)

Let us serve one another, as Jesus has served us.
They will know we are Christians by our love!
Let us love one another, as Jesus has loved us.
They will know we are Christians by our love!
Let us be disciples of Jesus' love.
They will know we are Christians by our love!

PRAISE SENTENCES (1 CORINTHIANS 11)

Christ is the Lamb of God!
Worship the Lamb!

Christ's body was broken for our salvation!
Worship the Lamb!
Christ's blood was poured out to seal us into God's love!
Worship the Lamb!

PRAISE SENTENCES (JOHN 13)

We are Jesus' disciples.
We worship the God of Love!
We are disciples of Jesus' love.
We worship the God of Love!
Jesus calls us his own.
We worship the God of Love!

OPENING PRAYER (EXODUS 12)

Ever-faithful God,
you beheld the bondage of your people in Egypt,
and hearkened to their cry.
When Pharaoh refused to let your people go,
you spared their firstborn,
that they would not suffer death for the sins of others.
When you chasten those who abuse and oppress
the helpless and voiceless in our day,
let your wrath once again pass over the righteous,
as it did in Egypt long ago.
When we seek to escape the chains of selfishness and
indifference that bind us, hasten to our aid,
that we may, in turn, aid those who suffer injustice.
We ask this in the name of your Son,
who called us to feed the hungry, clothe the naked,
and comfort the brokenhearted. Amen.

OPENING PRAYER (JOHN 13)

Eternal Christ,
as you washed the feet of your disciples
to show them the meaning of loving service,
wash clean our hearts,

that we may freely embrace your ministry
of service to others.
Help us keep your commandment to love one another,
that through our love, the world may know
that we are your disciples. Amen.

PRAYER OF CONFESSION (1 CORINTHIANS 11)

Eternal God, on this Holy Thursday, we remember that
Christ's body was broken for us, Christ's blood was
poured out for the forgiveness of our sins. We admit that
we do not like to remember the pain of Christ's sacrifice.
Forgive our forgetfulness. As we eat from the bread of
life, as we drink from the cup of salvation, help us honor
the gift of salvation offered to us. Amen.

BENEDICTION

We are washed clean by the One who washed the feet of
his disciples.
Christ has washed us clean.
We are blessed by the One who suffered the cross for our
salvation.
Christ has blessed us.
We are loved by the One who saved the world through
sacrificial love.
Christ has sealed us in his love.

APRIL 9, 2004

Good Friday

Mary J. Scifres

COLOR
Black or None

SCRIPTURE READINGS
Isaiah 52:13–53:12; Psalm 22; Hebrews 10:16-25; John 18:1–19:42

THEME IDEAS
The scriptures for this mournful day in the Christian year elicit themes of great sorrow: death, loneliness, suffering, and evil. The theme of sacrifice that arises, as we reflect on Jesus' death on the cross, reminds us that even the sorrows of this day are incomparable to the great love of God.

CALL TO WORSHIP
On this holy day of remembrance, we mourn the death of our Lord Jesus Christ.
We remember Christ's love.
On this holy day of sorrow, we grieve for the sins that cause God pain.
We remember Christ's suffering.
On this holy day of grief, we reflect on the little deaths we must die in order to follow Christ.
We remember Christ's teachings.
On this holy day of reflection, we listen for God's voice.

Open our ears that we might hear, even in the silence of this day.

CALL TO WORSHIP (HEBREWS 10)

Come into God's presence with hearts full of faith.
We come, with faithful hearts.
Come into God's presence, meeting together as the people of God.
We come, encouraging one another in love and goodness.
Come into God's presence, preparing for the day when Christ will come again.
We come, prepared for Christ's return as we create God's realm here and now.

PRAISE SENTENCES (PSALM 22)

Praise the Lord!
Glorify Christ's name throughout the earth.
Praise the Lord!
Praise the Lord!
Stand in awe before God's presence.
Praise the Lord!

CONTEMPORARY GATHERING WORDS

Come, children of God, and hear the story of Jesus' trial and death. Listen and know that God loves us.
God loves us!
God loves us!
God loves us!

CALL TO CONFESSION (ISAIAH 53)

Like sheep, we have all wandered from God. Let us turn back to God as we confess our sins before Christ.

PRAYER OF CONFESSION (ISAIAH 53)

Suffering Servant, forgive our sins and our transgressions. Cover our mistakes with your righteousness.

Perfect our intentions that they might fulfill your intentions for our lives. Lead us back to you when we stray from the path you have laid before us. In the name of the One who suffered on our behalf, we pray. Amen.

WORDS OF ASSURANCE (ISAIAH 53)

Christ, the righteous one, has borne our sins upon the cross. In the name of Christ, you are forgiven!
In the name of Christ, you are forgiven!

CALL TO CONFESSION (HEBREWS 10)

Approach God with a true heart. Come before Christ with faith in God's mercy. For Christ, who has promised mercy, is faithful and will hear our prayers.

PRAYER OF CONFESSION (HEBREWS 10)

Merciful God, we admit that we have not always listened when you have spoken your law in our thoughts. We have not always lived according to the love you have written on our hearts. We have doubted your forgiveness and turned away from our confession, in fear that your mercy had limits. Forgive our fickle minds, our hardened hearts, and our unfounded fears. Fill us with your mercy, and open our hearts and our minds, that we might love you and others with all our heart, mind, soul, and strength. Amen.

WORDS OF ASSURANCE (HEBREWS 10)

God has made a covenant through Christ Jesus—a covenant of love and mercy, a covenant to forgive our sinful thoughts and actions. Accept God's mercy, let Christ's love sprinkle us clean. Hold fast to our hope that is in Christ Jesus. Amen.

RESPONSIVE PRAYER

Christ Jesus, we know that your kingdom is not from this world.

We pray that your kingdom might come on earth as it is in heaven.

You came to testify to the truth.

We pray that your will might be done on earth as it is in heaven.

You call to us, and claim us when we abide in your truth.

Forgive us our sins as we forgive those who sin against us.

We know that you did not come for worldly glory.

But all honor and glory is yours, Christ Jesus, now and forevermore. Amen.

BENEDICTION

Remember this day, and keep it holy. Remember Christ's love, and make it precious in your heart. Remember Christ's sacrifice, and trust in God's grace. Amen.

APRIL 11, 2004

Easter Sunday

Brian Wren

COLOR
White

SCRIPTURE READINGS
Acts 10:34-43; Psalm 118:1-2, 14-24; 1 Corinthians 15:19-26; John 20:1-18 (or Luke 24:1-12)

THEME IDEAS
Step back a day. Only from the grief, loss, and despair of Easter Saturday can the resurrection be fully entered, or initial disbelief understood. Women are the first witnesses, disbelieved by the men (Luke 24:11), but here as always, God lifts up the lowly (Luke 1:52) and makes foundational a stone the official builders discard (Psalm 118:22). Christ's resurrection is an encounter with the incredible, appropriately praised with Psalm 118, sung from early Christian times as an Easter prophecy fulfilled. Christ's resurrection opens God's covenant to all (Acts 10:34-35), seals the guarantee of our deliverance from sin (without which we are still in our sins [1 Corinthians 15:17]), and opens the promise of life with God transcending life on earth, as each whole person ("body") is raised collectively with Christ (1 Corinthians 15:20).

CALL TO WORSHIP

With the church of Christ down the ages,
we share the Easter greeting:
"The Lord is risen!
He is risen indeed!"
From dryness and tears,
and the anguish of loss,
here is great good news:
"The Lord is risen!
He is risen indeed!"
From buried dreams,
and goodness destroyed,
here is great good news:
"The Lord is risen!
He is risen indeed!"
Over state-sponsored terror,
the power of the sword,
and the stranglehold of death,
"The Lord is risen!
He is risen indeed!"
Alleluia! Amen!

PRAISE SENTENCES (PSALM 118)

[For a shorter version, begin with "I shall not die, but I shall live."]

Leader	The Lord is my strength and my might,
All	**and has become my salvation.**
Leader	Listen! There are glad songs of victory in the tents of the righteous:
Voice 2	"The right hand of the LORD does valiantly!"
Voice 3	"The right hand of the LORD is exalted!"
Voice 4	"The right hand of the LORD does valiantly!"
Leader	I shall not die, but I shall live, and recount the deeds of the LORD.

All	**The stone that the builders rejected has become the chief cornerstone.**
Leader	This is the LORD's doing.
All	**It is marvelous in our eyes.**
Leader	This is the day that the LORD has made.
All	**Let us rejoice and be glad in it.**

CONTEMPORARY GATHERING WORDS

Today, of all days, if I say only "Good morning,"
and you say only *[give a gesture inviting the response]*
   "Good morning,"
it is not enough. It is not enough.
This good morning is God's best morning,
sunlight scattering darkness,
joy melting heartbreak,
life shattering death,
for Jesus Christ, God's shining light,
who was tortured, broken and buried,
is risen and alive in God,
alive among us, now, today, evermore, and always.
   Today's good morning
   is God's best morning.
   Alleluia! Amen.

CALL TO WORSHIP OR ACT OF PRAISE (ACTS 10, PSALM 118)

Here is a true story:
Jesus of Nazareth, sent from God,
filled with the power of the Spirit,
went about healing and doing good,
preaching peace to God's own people.
   Give thanks to the Living God,
   whose love persists forever.
Jesus was nailed to a tree,
executed, dead, and buried,
but God raised him from the dead.

> **The stone that the builders rejected**
> **has become the chief cornerstone.**
> Christ is appointed Savior and judge
> of living and dead,
> and everyone who believes in him
> receives forgiveness of sins through his name.
> **This is the work of the Living God.**
> **It is marvelous in our eyes.**

PRAYER

Living Christ, whose wondrous resurrection
fulfills, not a wish, but a promise,
unveil your presence among us,
that we may know in our hearts
and declare with our lips
that you are alive forevermore.

PRAYER

Risen Christ, whose first witnesses
were mocked and disbelieved,
convince us you are risen
through the lives of saints,
the words of scripture,
and the kindness of your people,
that in our steady witness
your glorious light may shine.

PRAYER

Outgoing God, we praise you
because through Jesus the Jew,
crucified and risen,
you offer full deliverance
to all earth's people.
Give us Easter vision,
that we may discover the world you love
through the eyes of the risen Christ.

PRAYER

Impartial God, we confess
that the best we can give unaided
is limited love to many
and wholehearted love to a few.
On this day of new beginnings
inspire us with your gospel
of wholehearted love for everyone
and limited love for none,
in the name of Jesus Christ.

CONTEMPORARY INVITATION TO COMMUNION

Here is good news: Jesus Christ is risen from the dead!
But it means that Jesus died,
and we don't want to think about death,
so please come back tomorrow.
The risen Christ says, follow me!
But life is filled with things to do,
people to love, and hopes to achieve,
so please come back tomorrow.
The risen Christ says, come to my table!
But that means spending our time
with people we'd rather not see,
so please come back tomorrow.
The risen Christ declares:
"*This* is the day that God has made,
therefore, rejoice and be glad in it!"
Then come, risen Christ,
and bring us to your table,
that through the fullness of life
to the finality of death
we may know your resurrection power. Amen.

BENEDICTION

As God's chosen witnesses,
we proclaim Jesus Christ.

As God's chosen witnesses
  we testify that Christ is risen.
As God's chosen witnesses
  may our behavior give evidence
  that Christ is alive among us.
May the peace of Christ be with you!
  And also with you!
Go in peace.

BENEDICTION

As we travel the Easter road,
Jesus Christ, alive in God,
can pinpoint where we are,
and help us navigate a new and better way.
Go then, on this week's journey of faith,
prepared for Christ to guide us
on highways or hidden roads
of peace-making, fair-dealing,
kindness, and forgiveness.
Christ is risen! Go in peace

Copyright © 2002 by Brian Wren

APRIL 18, 2004

Second Sunday of Easter

B. J. Beu

COLOR
White

SCRIPTURE READINGS
Acts 5:27-32; Psalm 150; Revelation 1:4-8; John 20:19-31

THEME IDEAS
Today's readings continue many of the great themes of Easter: resurrection, new life, and hope in the midst of profound fear and doubt. Revelation 1 deepens the theme of hope by making it clear that our hope in the resurrection is founded upon the One who was, and is, and is to come: the Alpha and Omega. John deepens our understanding of the possibilities that doubt afford in the life of faith. When doubting Thomas finds himself face-to-face with the risen Christ, he says: "My Lord and my God." Apathy, not doubt, is the opposite of faith. Doubt is an opportunity to dive deeper into our faith, and find our faith strengthened through the struggle.

CALL TO WORSHIP (PSALM 150)
Praise God in the sanctuary.
Praise God in the mighty firmament!
Praise God with trumpets.
Praise God with lute and harp!

Praise the Lord with tambourine and dance.
Praise the Lord with strings and pipes!
Praise God with clashing cymbals.
Praise God with beating drums.
Let everything that breathes praise the Lord!
Praise the Lord!

CALL TO WORSHIP

Behold, the Lord is coming!
We turn our eyes to the Lord!
Behold, the risen Christ is coming!
We turn our eyes to the Lord!
Behold, the One who is Alpha and Omega is coming!
We turn our eyes to the Lord!

CONTEMPORARY GATHERING WORDS (JOHN 20)

The risen Lord is among us!
We long to see and believe.
The risen Lord is among us!
We long to put aside all doubt.
The risen Lord is among us!
We long to proclaim:
"My Lord and my God!"

PRAISE SENTENCES

Christ is risen!
Alleluia!
Christ is risen!
Alleluia!
The Lord is risen!
Alleluia!

PRAISE SENTENCES (REVELATION 1)

Christ's love has healed us.
Christ's love has saved us!
Christ's love has set us free!

PRAISE SENTENCES (PSALM 150)

Blow the trumpets.
Christ is risen!
Clang the cymbals.
Christ is risen!
Dance, and play the tambourine.
Christ is risen!
Christ is risen!

OPENING PRAYER (JOHN 20)

God, your patient love is like a mighty glacier, slowly pushing aside all that stands before it. Be patient with us, as we strive to shore up our hesitant faith. Like Thomas, we want to believe in the power of your resurrection, but we have so many doubts. Hate often seems stronger than love. Death often seems stronger than life. Come to us, in the midst of our doubts, that we may see Christ's glory and proclaim with Thomas: "My Lord and my God!" Amen.

OPENING PRAYER (REVELATION 1)

Eternal God, who was, and is, and is to come, you are our Alpha and Omega, our beginning and ending. In you, O God, we move and have our being. Be the foundation of our strength, that no force may resist our efforts to bring your kingdom to earth. Be the foundation of our courage, that no threats may sway us from proclaiming your glory for all to hear. We ask this in the name of the One who conquered the grave to bring us eternal life. Amen.

BENEDICTION (JOHN 20)

The risen Lord has come among us!
We have seen and believe.
The risen Lord is among us still!
Faith has replaced our doubt.
The risen Lord goes with us as we leave this place.
Our Lord and our God goes with us.
Go with God's blessing.

APRIL 25, 2004

Third Sunday of Easter
Joel Emerson

COLOR
White

SCRIPTURE READINGS
Acts 9:1-6 (7-20); Psalm 30; Revelation 5:11-14; John 21:1-19

THEME IDEAS
Today's scriptures emphasize renewal and continual resurrection, and the praise and adoration we owe to the great God of healing and second chances. Whether it is Paul's conversion, the psalmist's healing, or Peter's restoration by Jesus to a sense of calling and mission, there are multiple opportunities in this worship context to focus on the resurrection, recovery, renewal, and rebirth of us all. We are challenged to be the instruments of this same resurrection, even in the lives of those we love the least, and fear the most. In Christ, redemption is for all people.

CALL TO WORSHIP (PSALM 30)
We exalt you Lord!
You have lifted us out of the depths!
We exalt you Lord!
You have heard our calls for help and have healed us!

We exalt you Lord!
You have brought us up from the grave!
We exalt you Lord!
You have spared us from going into the pit!
We exalt you Lord, and give you thanks forever!

CALL TO WORSHIP (REVELATION 5)

May we sing with the angels,
worthy is the Lamb who was slain to receive power!
May we sing with all creatures in heaven and earth,
worthy is the Lamb who was slain to receive wealth!
May we sing with the four living creatures of heaven,
worthy is the Lamb who was slain to receive
wisdom!
May we sing with the elders,
worthy is the Lamb who was slain to receive
strength!
Worthy is the Lamb who sits on the throne!
May we give God praise and honor, glory and power,
forever and ever! Amen!

CONTEMPORARY GATHERING WORDS (ACTS 9)

Welcome to the celebration
of the God of second chances.
Welcome to the celebration
of the God of hope and healing.
Welcome to the celebration
of the God of blinding love.
Come and join us as we sing our praises—
praises to the great God of new tomorrows
and forgiven yesterdays!

OPENING PRAYER

We praise you, O God, for your compassion and forgiveness. We ask your Spirit of hope and renewal to be present with us as we worship you, and sing of your worth

and love. Continue your work of resurrection in our lives. May we see the way clearly today, the way of our rebirth and renewal, through the resurrection of Jesus Christ. Amen.

PRAYER OF CONFESSION (ACTS 9)

O God, who blinded Saul on the road to Damascus for persecuting those who professed faith in your Son, we confess that we too have been blinded—blinded by ambition, blinded by greed, and blinded by selfishness. With eyes hidden from your light, we too have persecuted you with deeds done, and with deeds left undone. If this be sight, we pray that you would blind us anew. Blind us to our pride—a pride that allows us to look down on your children. Blind us to our shame—a shame that propels us to hurry past the ones who need your love the most. Blind us to our fear—a fear that keeps at arms length, those who are different from ourselves. Blind us with the light of your love, that the eyes of our hearts may be healed and see aright. Amen.

PRAYER OF RESPONSE TO THE WORD (JOHN 21)

God, we thank you that you greet us each morning and call us to be fishers of your people. We praise you for revealing your word to us today, a word of renewal and hope, a word of forgiveness and resurrection. We praise you that even though we have wasted much of our lives fishing on the wrong side of the boat, you gently correct us. Nothing in our lives is too sick, nothing has been going on too long, nothing is too addictive, or too shameful, or too sinful, that you cannot redeem us to be the people you call us to be. Empower us to take your transforming love to everyone we meet, that we might be an instrument of resurrection in their lives, as Jesus is in ours. Amen.

BENEDICTION

Let us go and find the people who live as if in the grave.

In Christ, we are resurrected. May we work for the resurrection of others.

Let us go and find the people who are suffering.

In Christ, we are recovered. May we work for the recovery of others.

Let us go and find the people who are tired.

In Christ, we are renewed. May we work for the renewal of others.

Let us go and find those who are lost.

In Christ, we are reborn. May we work for the rebirth of others.

Praise be to the God of second chances.

Amen!

MAY 2, 2004

Fourth Sunday of Easter
B. J. Beu

COLOR
White

SCRIPTURE READINGS
Acts 9:36-43; Psalm 23; Revelation 7:9-17; John 10:22-30

THEME IDEAS
The lections forward the theme that the resurrected
Christ is our one true shepherd—the shepherd spoken of
by the psalmist, who leads God's flock through fear and
trials to rest beside still waters; the shepherd spoken of in
John's Gospel and in the book of Revelation, who leads
God's flock to springs of eternal life, and who wipes
away every tear. Christ is our shepherd, and when we
hear and follow the call to follow the shepherd, we
belong to God's flock, and no one can snatch us from
God's hand.

CALL TO WORSHIP OR BENEDICTION (PSALM 23)
The Lord is our shepherd, we shall not want.
**Our shepherd makes us lie down in green pastures,
and leads us beside the still waters.**
The Lord restores our soul.
**Our shepherd leads us through the darkest valleys.
We shall fear no evil, for our shepherd is with us.**

Surely goodness and mercy shall follow us all the days of our lives,
and we shall dwell in the house of the Lord forever.

CALL TO WORSHIP (REVELATION 7)

The Lamb of God sits on heaven's throne.
Glory to the Lamb!
The Lamb of God is our shepherd, who leads us to springs of the water of life.
Glory to the Lamb!
Salvation belongs to our God and to the Lamb.
Glory to God and to the Lamb!

CONTEMPORARY GATHERING WORDS (JOHN 10)

Jesus is our shepherd.
We are his sheep.
The shepherd is calling us to join the flock.
We will follow our shepherd.
No one can snatch the sheep from the shepherd's hand.
In the shepherd's flock, we rest secure.

CONTEMPORARY GATHERING WORDS (ACTS 9)

Without Christ, we are dead to our sin.
In Christ, we are reborn to eternal life.
Praise God for the power of the resurrection.
We are here to praise God.

PRAISE SENTENCES (PSALM 23)

The Lord is our shepherd, we shall not want.
All praise to the shepherd!
Our shepherd makes us lie down in safety.
We praise the One in whom we rest secure!
Our shepherd leads us safely through trials of darkest fear.
All praise to the One who shields us from evil!

Goodness and mercy shall follow us all the days of our lives. And we shall dwell in the house of the Lord forever.
All praise to the shepherd!

PRAISE SENTENCES (REVELATION 7)
Worship the Lamb who sits on Heaven's throne.
Worship the Lamb!
Worship the Lamb who shelters us from harm.
Worship the Lamb!
Worship the Lamb who wipes away every tear.
Worship the Lamb!

OPENING PRAYER (ACTS 9)
Loving God, you have made your ways known through the teachings of your prophets, and through the life, death, and resurrection of your Son. We rejoice that the wonders Jesus performed continue on through the actions of his disciples. Just as Peter raised Tabitha from the dead, raise us also, O God, that we might rise above the numbness of our everyday lives, and become truly awake to the movement of your Spirit. Kindle in our hearts the passion to serve you as Christ's disciples, that the world may know that the resurrected One lives still. Amen.

OPENING PRAYER (JOHN 10, REVELATION 7)
Eternal Christ, before the foundations of the world were set, you sat on heaven's throne. In the fullness of time, you were born of Mary. And after your death and resurrection, you ascended to heaven to prepare a place for us. You are our true shepherd, and we are the sheep of your flock. Help us to hear your call and to follow your voice, that we might know the blessings of eternal life. May the works that you performed be known through us, that the world may see your flock here on earth, and through it, behold your glory. Amen.

PRAYER OF DEDICATION (ACTS 9)

We thank you, dear Lord, for the strength and joy that is embodied in your love. Let the miracles that your presence produces be evident in our living. We dedicate these gifts to miracle-making in Jesus Christ's name. Amen. (Sherry Parker)

BENEDICTION (PSALM 23, REVELATION 7)

The Shepherd has called us.
We hear and will follow the Shepherd.
The Shepherd has brought us to springs of eternal life.
We have tasted of its sweet waters.
The Shepherd walks with us in our need, and wipes away every tear.
We go with the protection of our Shepherd.
Go in peace.

MAY 9, 2004

Fifth Sunday of Easter/Mother's Day/
Festival of the Christian Home

Bea Barbara Soots

COLOR
White

SCRIPTURE READINGS
Acts 11:1-18; Psalm 148; Revelation 1:1-6; John 13:31-35

THEME IDEAS
The large sheet or tablecloth (Acts) symbolizes God's invitation to people of every culture to share in table fellowship with one another. The security of God dwelling with humanity (Revelation) and the call for disciples to be recognized by their love (John) provide rich contexts for worship. These scriptures, together with the celebrations of the Festival of the Christian Home and Mother's Day, call to mind at least two possible themes: Christian families and a call to nonviolence. The family theme should be inclusive of the variety of family systems in and around your area. The theme of nonviolence is based on Revelation and John, and on the first Mother's Day that was proclaimed by Julia Ward Howe in 1870. Howe called for an international gathering of women to mourn the war dead and to work together, that genuine peace might come to all.

CALL TO WORSHIP (ACTS 11)

The Holy One knits us together in one holy fabric.
Do not hinder God.

We come to worship the God who makes all of us clean.

God's baptism, through Jesus Christ,
provides the refreshing breeze of the Holy Spirit
for all who believe.
Do not hinder God.

We come to worship the God who offers us the gifts which lead to life: gifts of grace and repentance.

CONTEMPORARY GATHERING WORDS (JOHN 13)

God loves me.

God loves me.

All the time.

All the time.

All the time.

All the time.

God loves me.

God loves me.

God loves me.

God loves me.

All the time.

All the time.

PRAISE SENTENCES (PSALM 148)

Women and men, young and old together, families of all kinds:
Praise the Lord!

Praise the Lord!

Praise the Lord!

Praise the Lord!

With the mountains and hills, and with all God's creation, praise the Lord!

PRAISE SENTENCES (REVELATION 1, MOTHER'S DAY)

God, you live with us each day.
Your peace dwells among us.
Peace on Earth!
Peace on Earth!
Peace on Earth!
Blessed be your peace.

CONTEMPORARY GATHERING WORDS (REVELATION 1)

God dwells among us.
God lives with us!
We are God's holy people.
God lives with us!
Every tear has been dried.
God lives with us!
Death is no more.
God lives with us!
Mourning, crying, and pain are gone.
God lives with us!
Behold, a new heaven and a new earth;
the holy city, the new Jerusalem.
God lives with us!

PRAYER OF CONFESSION (ACTS 11, JOHN 13, MOTHER'S DAY)

Gracious and loving God, just as in Paul's time, Gentiles were "alien" to Jews, too often we isolate ourselves from those who are "other" in our midst, even from those in our own families. We hinder your creation, and defile those whom you have made holy. Hold us, dear God, in your loving embrace. Rock us in your loving care, that we may grow as your disciples. Lead us to love each other, even as you have loved us. Amen.

TIME WITH CHILDREN (MOTHER'S DAY)

On this day, I ask the children if they know what is special about this particular Sunday. Then I ask if they have given their mothers a present yet. No matter how they answer, I tell of another gift that I believe every child can give—a gift that I know every mother and parent will appreciate: a promise to practice nonviolence.

MOTHER'S DAY PROMISE FOR TIME WITH CHILDREN

I want to be like Jesus. I promise not to hit, kick, or hurt in any way my brothers, sisters, friends, or classmates, no matter how angry I feel. Amen.

BENEDICTION (REVELATION 1, JOHN 13)

Let peace dwell among us so that we might become God's family of faithful disciples, loving one another, even as God loves us.

MAY 16, 2004

Sixth Sunday of Easter

B. J. Beu

COLOR
White

SCRIPTURE READINGS
Acts 16:9-15; Psalm 67; Revelation 21:1-10, 22–22:5; John 14:23-29

THEME IDEAS
Easter is a time for sheer delight, a time to praise God with renewed faith and with new vision. Psalm 67 invites us to open our hearts and to praise God for saving us, guiding us, and blessing us. The reading from Revelation provides a deeper sense of God's saving power. There will be a new heaven and a new earth, and the nations will walk in the light of the Lamb of God. Mourning and weeping will be no more, for God will wipe away every tear. The Gospel of John further comforts our sense of loss at Christ's departure. Because God has sent us the Advocate, the Holy Spirit, to bring us peace, take away our fear, and lead us into truth, we will never be alone on our spiritual journey.

CALL TO WORSHIP (PSALM 67)
Let the peoples praise you, O God.
Let all the peoples praise you!

Let the nations be glad and sing for joy.
For you judge the peoples with justice and truth!
God, our God, has blessed us.
Let all the ends of the earth revere the living God!
Let the peoples praise you, O God.
Let all the peoples praise you!

CALL TO WORSHIP (REVELATION 21)

Behold, the glory of God comes.
There will be a new heaven and a new earth.
We worship the One who makes all things new!
Behold, the throne of God comes.
God will dwell with us, and take away our suffering and pain.
We worship the One who wipes away every tear!
Behold, the light of God comes. The Lamb of God will be our light, and darkness will be no more.
We worship the One whose glory is our light!

CONTEMPORARY GATHERING WORDS OR PRAISE SENTENCES (PSALM 67)

Sing and shout for joy. God is worthy to be praised.
O God, we sing your praises.
Sing and shout for joy. Our mighty God has blessed us.
O God, we sing your praises.
Sing and shout for joy.
God is worthy to be praised.
O God, we sing your praises.

PRAISE SENTENCES OR BENEDICTION (EASTER)

Hear the good news. Christ is risen!
Praise the One who conquers death!
Hear the good news. Christ is risen!
Praise the One who brings us life!
Hear the good news. Christ has risen!
Praise the One who leads us home!

PRAISE SENTENCES (JOHN 14)

Christ's words are true.
Teach us Holy Spirit!
Christ's words bring life.
Teach us Holy Spirit!
Christ is speaking still.
Teach us Holy Spirit!

OPENING PRAYER (ACTS 16)

Great Spirit, you come to us in visions and dreams, calling us beyond the narrow confines of our waking perceptions. As you opened the heart of Lydia before us, open our hearts, that we might understand Christ's teaching, and share the living Christ with those we meet. As you guided Paul's footsteps around the shores of the Mediterranean Sea, guide our footsteps on our journey, that we may go where you send us, and share the good news of Jesus Christ with all those who seek you. Amen.

OPENING PRAYER (REVELATION 21)

O God, our lamp and our light, we praise you that you do not leave us in darkness. Grant us the vision to see within this world of pain, the new heaven and new earth that is within our midst when we live as your holy people. Help us to faithfully become the Body of Christ in our community, wiping away each other's tears, even as we anticipate the time when you will dwell among us, and wipe away every tear. Let us behold the light of your glory, that we will need neither sun nor moon to guide us. We pray this in the name of the Lamb of God—the One who is our true light. Amen.

BENEDICTION (JOHN 14)

Jesus said: "Peace I leave with you; my peace I give to you."
In Christ, we have found peace.

Jesus said: "Do not let your hearts be troubled, and do not let them be afraid."

In Christ, we have no fear.

Christ has come to us, blessing us with eternal life.

In Christ, we are alive.

BENEDICTION (PSALM 67)

May God be gracious to us, and bless us,
and make his face to shine upon us.

We go with God's light to lead us.

May God be gracious to us, and bless us,
and grant us peace.

We go with God's peace to sustain us.

MAY 23, 2004

Seventh Sunday of Easter/ Ascension Sunday

Mary J. Scifres

COLOR
White

ASCENSION SUNDAY READINGS
Acts 1:1-11; Psalm 47; Ephesians 1:15-23; Luke 24:44-53

SEVENTH SUNDAY OF EASTER READINGS
Acts 16:16-34; Psalm 97; Revelation 22:12-14, 16-17, 20-21; John 17:20-26

THEME IDEAS
The Ascension Sunday scriptures celebrate the majesty and power of God and the promise to those who hold fast to their faith in Jesus Christ. God has raised Christ from the dead and subjected all things to him. Christ's ascension into heaven is not a moment to be mourned, but an occasion to be celebrated, for believers will now be blessed by the power of the Holy Spirit, and the saints will share in Christ's glory. The Easter scriptures also celebrate the majesty and power of God, but here, the power is more ominous. The power of God entails judgment, and those who pit themselves against God's purposes should beware. The same power that created earth and sea is

present in Christ, and those who align themselves against God's righteousness will smart for it. Christ's good news for the faithful is also a warning to the ungodly.

CALL TO WORSHIP (PSALM 47, PSALM 97)
Clap your hands and shout with joy.
The Lord our God is king!
Clap your hands and sing with praise.
The Lord our God is love!
Clap your hands as the trumpet sounds.
The Lord our God is here!
Clap your hands and worship God.

CALL TO WORSHIP (REVELATION 22)
The Spirit of God says, "Come!"
Let everyone who hears come.
The Spirit of God says, "Welcome!"
Let everyone who is thirsty come.
The Spirit of God says, "Drink!"
Let everyone drink from the water of life and be filled.

CONTEMPORARY GATHERING WORDS (PSALM 47)
Clap your hands and shout with joy.
Praise the Lord, Most High!
Clap your hands and sing with praise.
Praise the Lord, Most High!

PRAISE SENTENCES (ACTS 16)
Believe in the Lord Jesus Christ and you will be saved!
We believe in Christ!

PRAISE SENTENCES (PSALM 47)
Sing praise to God!
Clap your hands with joy!
Shout for all to hear!
God is the king of all!

Sing praise to God!
We'll sing God's praises!
Sing praise to God!
We'll sing God's praises!

PRAISE SENTENCES OR BENEDICTION (REVELATION 22)

Jesus said, "See I am coming soon!"
Surely Christ is coming soon!

OPENING PRAYER (LUKE 24, EPHESIANS 1)

Open our minds, Spirit of Wisdom,
 that we might understand your Word.
As the scriptures are read,
 let us sense your presence,
 as you blow through our midst.
Bless us with your presence here,
 even as you are seated in the highest heavens.
Amen.

OPENING PRAYER (JOHN 17)

Loving Christ, help us to become one,
 as we worship you in spirit and truth.
Let this time of worship give us a sense of unity
 that will show the world your gracious acceptance
 of all people.
Grant us your light,
 that the world may see your glory
 shining through our lives.
Bless us with your love,
 that the world may know your loving presence.
Amen.

CALL TO PRAYER (EPHESIANS 1)

I have heard of your faith in Christ Jesus
 and your love for all of God's people.

For this reason, I give thanks without ceasing
and remember you in my prayers.
Let us remember one another as we pray together.

PRAYER OF THE PEOPLE (EPHESIANS 1)

Glorious God, we offer you our thanks and praise,
as we pray for a world in need.
We give you thanks for this church and its members. . . .
We ask your blessing on the many saints of this world. . . .
We pray for a faith that fills us with hope. . . .
We pray for a spirit of wisdom and truth. . . .
We pray for eyes and hearts
that see this world as you see it. . . .
We pray for a hope that never ends. . . .
We pray for your power to rule our lives,
and guide our world. . . .
In the name of Christ Jesus,
risen from the dead and seated on high. Amen.

BENEDICTION (EPHESIANS 1)

May the God of all glory give you a spirit of wisdom.
May the Christ of all grace give you the knowledge of
truth. May the Spirit of all love open your eyes, that you
will know the hope to which God has called us. May this
body of Christ go forth to show the hope of God's glory,
love, and grace to all the world.

BENEDICTION (LUKE 24)

We are the witnesses of Christ Jesus.
We go forth to share Christ's good news with all.
We have seen and heard God's Word.
We go forth to share God's word with all.
We are filled with the Holy Spirit.
**We go forth with the Spirit's blessing,
today and all days. Amen.**

MAY 30, 2004

Pentecost Sunday
Bill Hoppe

COLOR
Red

SCRIPTURE READINGS
Acts 2:1-21; Psalm 104:24-34, 35*b*; Romans 8:14-17; John 4:8-17 (25-27)

THEME IDEAS
Pentecost, also called the Feast of Weeks, the Feast of Harvest, or the Feast of First-Fruits, was observed by the Hebrew people on the fiftieth day after Passover (Deuteronomy 16:9-12). In the lesson from the Acts of the Apostles, Pentecost is marked by the manifestation of the Holy Spirit, sounding like a great wind and appearing as tongues of fire. It also symbolizes the birthday of the church and the beginning of a spiritual harvest (Matthew 9:37-38), as the good news of Christ's resurrection is proclaimed publicly for the first time by the apostles. This is a day to celebrate the presence of the Holy Spirit among us, our promised Advocate (John 14:16-17), and to "rekindle the gift of God that is within [us] . . . for God did not give us a spirit of cowardice, but rather a spirit of power and of love and of self-discipline" (2 Timothy 1:6-7).

CALL TO WORSHIP (ACTS 2, JOHN 14, PENTECOST)

In rushing wind, in cleansing fire,
come, Holy Spirit, come!
In silence, in your quiet, still voice,
come, Holy Spirit, come!
As our Advocate, as our Comforter,
come, Holy Spirit, come!
Spirit of life and of grace, spirit of Christ and of promise,
come, Holy Spirit, come!
That we may worship you in spirit and in truth,
come, Holy Spirit, come!

CALL TO WORSHIP OR CONTEMPORARY GATHERING WORDS (ROMANS 8)

All who are led by the Spirit are the children of God!
We are God's children!
We have received the spirit of adoption, not of slavery!
We are God's children!
The Holy Spirit bears witness!
We are God's children!
We are God's heirs, and joint heirs with Christ!
All glory and praise to God!

PRAISE SENTENCES (ROMANS 8, EPHESIANS 1, 1 PETER 4)

The Spirit of life in Christ Jesus has set us free!
We are sealed with the Spirit of promise! The Spirit of
God dwells within us! We are blessed. The Spirit of glory
and of God rests upon us!

OPENING PRAYER (PENTECOST)

Dear Lord, thank you for bringing us together in worship
this day. Thank you for your open and loving arms, welcoming us here as your family, calling us to be your

church. Your love touches us all, leaving no one bereft of your presence. Together, we form the body of Christ, each of us playing an important role in your divine plan. Fill us with your Spirit. Rekindle your gifts within us. Thank you for making all things possible through Jesus, in whose name we pray. Amen.

OPENING PRAYER (ROMANS 8, GALATIANS 5)

By the Holy Spirit, O Lord, anoint us with your oil of gladness; fill us with your living water; ignite your fire within us! Equip us for every good work. Through your Spirit, may we bring forth a harvest of love, joy, peace, patience, kindness, generosity, faithfulness, gentleness, and self-control—fruits of the abundant life you have given us in Christ Jesus. Amen.

PRAYER OF CONFESSION (PENTECOST)

Lord, in the flames of adversity, you have tested us, proved us, refined us. Our souls are cleansed and purified as the fire of the Holy Spirit burns away all that falls short of God's glory. O great firewind of God, purify us like silver, refine us like gold. Make us vessels fit to be filled with your Spirit! In your grace and mercy, in your true love, give us pure hearts and a steadfast and willing spirit. Revive within us the joy of your deliverance and salvation! Amen.

BENEDICTION (ISAIAH 61, LUKE 4, REVELATION 2)

Let us bring the good news to the afflicted!
The Spirit of the Lord is upon us!
Let all broken hearts be mended. Let all wounds be healed!
The Spirit of the Lord is upon us!
Let all captive souls be set free. Let blind eyes be made to see!

The Spirit of the Lord is upon us!
Let joy pour down like rain. Let there be no more tears,
no more pain!
The Spirit of the Lord is upon us!
Let us live for the year of our Lord!
The Spirit of the Lord is upon us!

JUNE 6, 2004

Trinity Sunday
B. J. Beu

COLOR
White

SCRIPTURE READINGS
Proverbs 8:1-4, 22-31; Psalm 8; Romans 5:1-5; John 16:12-15

THEME IDEAS
Running throughout the day's scripture readings is the delight God takes in the human race. During the creation of the inhabited world, Wisdom rejoiced before God, taking delight in the human race. The psalmist marvels that amidst the wonders of creation, human beings were created but a little lower than God. Paul boasts of our hope to share in God's glory, through the love poured out to us in the Holy Spirit. And John declares that this same Spirit will lead us into all truth. Despite any feelings of worthlessness we might harbor for ourselves, God delights in leading us into the fullness of life.

CALL TO WORSHIP (PSALM 8)
O Lord, our God, how majestic is your name in all the earth.
Your glory shines above the heavens.
We behold the works of your fingers: the moon and the stars sing your praises.

What are human beings that you are mindful of us?
Yet you have made us a little lower than God.
You have crowned us with glory and honor.
O Lord, our God, how majestic is your name in all the earth.

CONTEMPORARY GATHERING WORDS (PROVERBS 8)

Wisdom calls to us, "Rejoice and delight in the Lord!"
We rejoice and delight in the Lord.
Delight in the Lord, whose love is as deep as the sea.
We rejoice and delight in the Lord.
Rejoice in the Lord, whose righteous will guides and leads us.
We rejoice and delight in the Lord.
Rejoice and delight in the Lord, for God's mercy never ends.
We rejoice and delight in the Lord.

PRAISE SENTENCES (PROVERBS 8)

Wisdom rejoices in the work of God's hands.
Our delight is in the Lord!
Wisdom rejoices in the splendor of God's handiwork.
Our delight is in the Lord!
All praise to the Wisdom of God.
Our delight is in the Lord!

PRAISE SENTENCES (PSALM 8)

God's name is above all names.
The works of God are a wonder to behold.
God fills us with glory.
Praise God's holy name!

OPENING PRAYER (ROMANS 5)

Eternal God, foundation of our faith, you have granted us peace through your Son, Jesus Christ. When we live faithfully, and embrace the road to the cross, you bestow upon us your glory. In our suffering, grant us endurance. In our endurance, grant us strength of character. Through strength of character, grant us hope, that we may know the love you pour out to us in the Holy Spirit. Amen.

OPENING PRAYER (PSALM 8, JOHN 16)

Great Spirit, we behold your glory in the starry heavens and in the wonders of earth and sea. Who are we that you care for us so deeply, and love us so completely? May our actions reflect the glory and honor you bestow upon us. Come into our lives, gentle Spirit, and lead us into truth, that our lives might be a beacon to those who have lost their way. Amen.

PRAYER OF CONFESSION (JOHN 16)

Spirit of Truth, we confess that we have not always listened to what you would teach us. We have trusted in our own wisdom, rather than waiting patiently for the fullness of truth that you alone can reveal to us. In our failure to be still and listen, we have missed the glory of Christ that you bring. Forgive our inattention, and lead us into truth, that we may bear witness to our risen Lord. Amen.

ASSURANCE OF PARDON (ROMANS 5)

Trust in the Lord, for God's promises are sure. Hope in the Lord, for God's love has been poured into our hearts through the Holy Spirit. Through God's life-giving Spirit, we are forgiven. Amen!

BENEDICTION (PROVERBS 8, PSALM 8, ROMANS 5, JOHN 16)

Go with the blessings of the Holy Spirit.
God's Spirit will lead us into truth.
Go with the joy of being God's children.
God's Wisdom will be our delight.
Go with the grace and peace of our Lord, Jesus Christ.

JUNE 13, 2004

Second Sunday After Pentecost
Judy Schultz

COLOR
Green

SCRIPTURE READINGS
1 Kings 21:1-21*a*; Psalm 5:1-8; Galatians 2:15-21; Luke 7:36–8:3

THEME IDEAS
God is present and hears us morning after morning, day after day. Our self-centeredness, like the greed of King Ahab and the codependence of his wife Jezebel, can eclipse our experience of God's presence. We can substitute things for the Holy God, and even make special persons in our lives into idols. Yet God forgives us again and again. We are freed from the rigidity of the law by the grace of God and enabled to live through the gift of faithfulness, seen fully in Jesus Christ. Like the woman who wept and anointed the feet of Jesus, we are called to live lives of self-giving and deep gratitude.

CALL TO WORSHIP (PSALM 5)
This morning, O God, hear our voices.
This morning, O God, we raise our voices to you.
Trusting in the abundance of your love, we enter your house.

We bow down in awe and worship before you.
Lead us, O Lord, in your righteousness.
Make your ways clear before us.

CALL TO WORSHIP (GALATIANS 2)

We come this morning with joy, to worship God.
We do not come to justify ourselves.
For you, O God, do not judge us by our righteousness,
but you accept us as we are, out of your great love.
We come with joy to worship you.
We come with grateful hearts to worship you.

CALL TO WORSHIP (GALATIANS 2)

Come worship God!
We come gladly to worship God!
Come worship God in freedom!
We come freely, knowing God welcomes us!
For we are freed of the law's requirement,
We are free to trust God's powerful grace.
We have known the power of grace in our lives.
We come thankfully and faithfully to worship!

CONTEMPORARY GATHERING WORDS (GALATIANS 2)

Christ lives in us!
We live by faith in the Son of God!
We rejoice in our new life.
Christ lives in us!
Christ lives in us!
We live by faith in Christ.
We live by faith!
We live by faith indeed!
Let us sing our praises to the One who lives in us!

PRAISE SENTENCES (PSALM 5)

God hears our cries and all our sighing.
Every morning, every day, God hears our voices.

Because of God's steadfast love,
 we are always welcome in God's presence.
God will lead us in the ways of all righteousness.
Praise God for God's love and gentle leading!

PRAISE SENTENCES (GALATIANS 2)

We know you welcome us!
Your love makes us worthy!
We believe in your Son Jesus.
Through him, you have raised us to new life.
Praise God for the gift of the Son!

OPENING PRAYER (LUKE 7-8)

Gracious and holy God,
 we give you thanks for your boundless,
 lavishly forgiving love.
We are not worthy to come into your presence,
 but your grace makes us worthy.
We pour out our hearts to you
 like the woman pouring costly perfume
 from the alabaster jar.
We bow before you, as she did,
 with hearts overflowing with gratitude and love.
Amen.

OPENING PRAYER (PSALM 5)

Wondrous Spirit, we come into your holy presence
 knowing that you receive us gladly and eagerly.
Morning by morning, you listen for us,
 and morning by morning our hearts leap up to you.
Grace our lives with your presence this day.
Hold us in your hands, lead us in your ways,
 and keep us in your love. Amen.

PRAYER OF CONFESSION (1 KINGS)

O Holy God, we confess that, like King Ahab,
 we see and desire what is not rightfully ours.

Like Queen Jezebel,
>   we have plotted to obtain what we desired
>   without regard to what is right.
Forgive our restlessness and discontent with what we have.
Forgive our unquenchable thirst for more commodities.
Forgive our disregard for the right of others
>   to have possessions greater than our own.
Teach us temperance and patience, O God,
>   and teach us to be satisfied with the gifts of your Spirit.
In the name of your Son Jesus, we pray. Amen.

UNISON PRAYER (1 KINGS 21, LUKE 7)

Loving God, Creator of opportunity and choice,
Giver of justice and mercy,
>   we pray that our choices
>   might reflect our life in you.
Where we have sinned,
>   lead us to repentance.
Where we have repented,
>   help us to acknowledge your mercy.
Where we have accepted your mercy,
>   free us to pass it on to others.
We worship you in the name of Jesus Christ
>   who embodied your justice and love.
Amen. (Sherry Parker)

BENEDICTION

May we go forth, led by God!
>   **Lead us, O God, in your righteousness.**
Make your ways clear before us.
>   **Guide us in the ways that lead to truth.**
Go with us each step of the way, O God.
>   **Be our companion and our guide.**
May we go forth rejoicing,
>   **knowing that God goes before us and with us.**

JUNE 20, 2004

Third Sunday After Pentecost/ Father's Day
Robert Blezard

COLOR

Green

SCRIPTURE READINGS

1 Kings 19:1-15*a*; Psalm 42; Galatians 3:23-29; Luke 8:26-39

THEME IDEAS

When we are distressed, confused, burdened, overwhelmed, and frightened, God is our comfort. Even the mightiest of God's prophets, Elijah, is not immune to emotional distress. After delivering miracles and signs and wonders in the name of Yahweh, Elijah is smitten by fear, confusion, and self-doubt. In the wilderness he receives food and comfort. Psalm 42 reaffirms that God, whose love and songs refresh us, is the source of healing for downcast souls. God desires to lead us out of confusion's darkness into the light of clarity, as shown in Jesus' deliverance of the man possessed by demons that made him insane. Patriarchal images of God need no reinforcement in our religious culture, but today—Father's Day—it seems appropriate to remember that God is our heavenly father who loves and comforts us as an earthly father would in our common, human suffering.

CALL TO WORSHIP (1 KINGS 19:1-15A)

Lord, your children are weary.
God, give us your rest.
Your children are hungry.
God, give us your food.
Your children are thirsty.
God, give us your holy water.
Your children are overwhelmed.
God, give us your strength.
Your children are confused.
God, give us your wisdom.
Your children are frightened.
God, give us your courage.
Your children are disheartened.
God, give us your inspiration.
Your children are scattered.
God, gather us together,
and hold us in your holy, loving arms.

CALL TO WORSHIP (PSALM 42)

As a deer pants for streams of water,
so our souls pant for you, O God.
Our souls thirst for the living God.
Wet our lips with your living waters, O God.
To God we open our downcast souls.
Refresh us with your love and your songs.
To God we direct all our hurts and hopes.
You are the source of our hope and our salvation.

CONTEMPORARY GATHERING WORDS

We come to God's house, not as guests but as family.
As children of God, we receive God's blessing.

Through our faith in Jesus Christ, we are God's sons and daughters.
As children of God, we receive God's blessing.
The feast is prepared, the candles are lit, the music plays.
As children of God, we receive God's blessing.
God gives us the bread of life for our hungry hearts.
As children of God, we receive God's blessing.
God pours out living water for our thirsty souls.
As children of God, we receive God's blessing.
Here we find respite from our busy, hectic lives.
As children of God, we receive God's blessing.

PRAISE SENTENCES

We are God's daughters and sons! We are heirs! We are family! God takes care of our every need. Let us rejoice in the lives that God our Father has given us!

PRAISE SENTENCES

When I'm down and troubled,
I will call upon the Lord.
God dries my tear-streaked face.
I will call upon the Lord.
God comforts all my sorrows.
I will call upon the Lord.
God wraps me in loving arms.
I will call upon the Lord.
God makes my future bright.
I will call upon the Lord.
God is always there for me.
I will call upon the Lord.

OPENING PRAYER (GALATIANS 3:23-29)

God of love and healing, you freed us from our chains by revealing the way of faith in Jesus Christ. Through our baptism, you accepted us as your sons and daughters and clothed us in the love of Christ. We welcome your presence as we lift our lives to you, and open our souls to your renewing Spirit, through Jesus Christ, our Lord. Amen.

OPENING PRAYER (FATHER'S DAY)

Like a loving father, you cherish us unconditionally, you discipline us with gentleness, you feed and clothe us, you tend to our every need. We thank you for your many blessings and welcome your Spirit in our midst. May we be refreshed by your loving, healing presence. Amen.

PRAYER OF CONFESSION

God, we confess that through our sin we have made a mess, not only of our world, but of our lives. In our blindness, we fail to see beyond our narrow self-interest. In our deafness, we choose to hear neither your words of guidance and comfort, nor the cries of the impoverished and oppressed all around us. In our dumbness, we fill our mouths with foolish trivialities instead of truth and love. In our madness, we convince ourselves we are on the right path, though deep inside we know it leads to death. For these sinful choices, we bear the pain of empty souls, the false satiation of consumption, the isolation of relationships unmade, the confusion of mixed values. But you are the God of mercy, eager to receive penitent hearts. Help us to see, help us to hear, help us to speak and live your truth. We pray your forgiveness and pledge ourselves to healing the brokenness all around us. Through Jesus Christ our Lord. Amen.

PRAYER OF CONFESSION

Your world is full of woe and strife, and we share the blame. Seeking to assure first our own financial, emotional, and physical security, we have closed our ears and eyes—and ultimately our hearts—to our brothers and sisters in need, and perpetuated economic oppression, hunger, and disease. Our silence and inaction have made us co-conspirators of injustice. We who have been made free have failed to unchain those around us. We pray for your forgiveness, seek your renewal, thirst for your inspiration, and delight in another chance. In Jesus' name we pray. Amen.

BENEDICTION (1 KINGS 19:1-15A)

May the God who is revealed, not in the ferocious wind, not in the earthquake, or even the fire, but in a hushed whisper be with you, comfort you, feed you, and commission you for mighty deeds.

JUNE 27, 2004

Fourth Sunday After Pentecost
Mary J. Scifres

COLOR
Green

SCRIPTURE READINGS
2 Kings 2:1-2, 6-14; Psalm 77:1-2, 11-20; Galatians 5:1, 13-25; Luke 9:51-62

THEME IDEAS
During the ordinary season, a single theme is hard to find in scripture readings that run chronologically, rather than thematically. But the above lessons offer us an opportunity to weave together a lesson of discipleship or Spirit-filled guidance. The discipleship displayed by Elisha and Jesus' challenging words in Luke are vivid reminders that following God often brings pain and rejection. The spirit that Elisha desires is none other than the Spirit of God that bears fruit (Galatians).

CALL TO WORSHIP (2 KINGS 2)
We come, seeking God's face.
Send your Spirit into this place.
We enter into this Holy of Holies for a time of worship.
Send your Spirit into our time together.
We gather as your people.
Send your Spirit into our lives.

CALL TO WORSHIP (PSALM 77)

Seek the Lord and the way of God.
For the way of God is holy.
Remember God's wonders and the gifts of God's grace.
For the works of God are mighty.
Live by the grace of God.
**For the redemption of God is promised
and fulfilled in Christ's strength and mercy.**
Let us worship the Holy One of strength and mercy.
Amen.

CALL TO WORSHIP (GALATIANS 5)

For freedom Christ has set us free.
Let us stand firm and resist slavery to sin.
By the Holy Spirit we are called to bear fruit—
love, joy, peace, patience, kindness, generosity,
faithfulness, gentleness, and self-control.
**We gather now, trusting in the saving power of Jesus
Christ.**
We desire to live by the Holy Spirit. (Sherry Parker)

CONTEMPORARY GATHERING WORDS

We come to worship a God of wonders.
Our God is a mighty God!
We come to worship a God of mercy.
Our God is a mighty God!
We come to worship a God of miracles.
Our God is a mighty God!
We come to worship a God of love.
Our God is a mighty God!

OPENING SENTENCES

Seek the Lord. Seek the Lord.
Seek the Holy One of Israel!

OPENING PRAYER (2 KINGS 2, GALATIANS 5)

Let your Spirit guide our time together. As we worship, blow over us with your wisdom and your guidance. Enter into our hearts and our lives, that we might be changed. Spirit of truth and justice, be with us now. Amen.

PRAYER OF CONFESSION (GALATIANS 5)

Forgive us, Holy Spirit, for our self-indulgent behaviors.
Forgive us when we spread cruelty, instead of love.
Forgive us our human sins of impurity and idolatry.
Forgive us when we bring strife and jealousy into relationships that yearn for peace and understanding.
Forgive us when our anger brings dissensions and division.
Fill us with your Spirit, that we might bring
   love and joy into our relationships,
   peace and patience into your world,
   kindness and generosity into our community,
   faithfulness and strength into your church,
   gentleness and self-control into our daily lives.
Through your gracious Spirit, we pray. Amen.

WORDS OF ASSURANCE (GALATIANS 5)

For freedom Christ has set us free. Stand firm, dear friends, against the slavery that sin brings into our lives. We are called to freedom—freedom to love our neighbors as ourselves. God gives us this freedom through the power of Christ's forgiveness. Accept this gift, and live in this freedom as God's beloved ones!

PRAYER OF RESPONSE (2 KINGS)

God of wind and flame, send us a double share of your Spirit. As Elisha before us, help us to yearn for your flames of justice, and your winds of wisdom. Give us the Spirit of passion and commitment that brings your realm into being. Grant us these gifts that we might be your prophets of today, bringing hope for the world of tomorrow. Amen.

Closing Prayer (Luke)

Christ Jesus, you have walked this path of life before us. You know the lonely road we travel. Help us to follow you without turning back. Guide our steps, that we might walk in your ways. Strengthen our resolve, that we might be the disciples you desire us to be. In your holy name, we pray. Amen.

Blessing (Galatians 5)

As you go forth, live by the Spirit, that you may know the fruit of that life.
May God bless you with these gifts:
Love—that others may know
    Christ's grace shining through you.
Joy—that others may see the glory
    of the gospel in your face.
Peace—that others may sense God's
    centering guidance in your life.
Patience—that others may find serenity
    in your presence.
Kindness—that others may know
    Christ's compassion through you.
Generosity—that God's world
    might become a better place.
Faithfulness—that Christ might find
    in you a true disciple.
Gentleness—that others may sense God's
    love in you.
Self-control—that you may find satisfaction
    in your actions and decisions.
Go forth with the power and blessing of the Holy Spirit.

BENEDICTION (GALATIANS 5, LUKE 9)

Let us live by the Spirit,
that we may also be guided by the Spirit.
Go forth in God's Spirit.
We will follow where Christ leads,
without ever turning back.

JULY 4, 2004

Fifth Sunday After Pentecost
John Brewer

COLOR
Green

SCRIPTURE READINGS
2 Kings 5:1-14; Psalm 30; Galatians 6:(1-6) 7-16; Luke 10:1-11, 16-20

THEME IDEAS
The kingdom of God is closer than we think. To the extent that we anticipate it, God's kingdom becomes tangibly present to us when we see change and transformation taking place. In spite of our fear of change, we discover the freedom of the future only by leaving the past behind. By braving the perils of "death to our past," we enter the freedom of God's new beginning.

CALL TO WORSHIP (2 KINGS 5)
Come, be cleansed of all that binds us to our brokenness.
We shall be free!
Cleansed by God, who can hold us in the chains of yesterday's sins?
We shall be free!
Here in the presence of God's flowing grace, we can overcome all fear!
We shall be free of our fear and doubt.

We are invited to know wholeness. Do you so believe?
By faith, we will immerse ourselves today in the love of God, a love that leads to our own healing and wholeness!
Then let us gather in anticipation and great hope. For we shall know a new freedom from our fears and doubts!
Let everyone give thanks and praise to our God!
Let everyone praise God for the Spirit of Christ!

GATHERING WORDS (LUKE 10)

Together, we gather to receive the power of God!
Together, we are empowered to do the works of God!
Together, we gather to hear the voice of God!
Together, we can share the labor and love of God!
Together, we shall see the power of God's Spirit in our midst!
Together, we shall bring peace to replace conflict.
Together, we shall overcome the perils in the world.
Together, we shall see our names written in heaven!
Together, we shall give thanks and praise to God, for the power of Spirit and Life.
Together, we shall lift our voices, and sing to the glory of God!

CALL TO WORSHIP (PSALMS 30)

I will exalt you, O Lord!
For you lifted me out of the depths!
O Lord my God, I called to you for help,
and you healed me!
Sing to the Lord, you saints; praise God's holy name.
For God's anger lasts only a moment, but the Lord's favor lasts a lifetime.
Hear, O Lord, and be merciful to me.
You turned my wailing into dancing!
You removed my sackcloth, and clothed me with joy!

My heart will sing to you and not be silent.
O Lord, my God, I will give you thanks forever!
O Lord, my God, I will give you thanks forever!

OPENING PRAYER

O God who never changes, we come before you on this day, to seek the change that only you can bring to our wounded hearts and broken spirits. From the bumps and bruises we receive through daily living, we come to this place and time to be transformed, cleansed, and healed. O Lord who was and is and is to come, give us faith to become more fully the reflections of your love you have called us to become. Breathe on us the Breath of transforming life, the Holy Spirit of Christ Jesus. We gather in anticipation of your work in our lives. Amen.

OPENING PRAYER

O Lord God of freedom, we gather for worship and direction. Chains and walls and locks and burdens hinder our knowing freedom in your Spirit. Come to us now, as we come to you. Help us to know how to find release from those physical and mental prisons we have established in the midst of our fear and doubt. Open the gates of our minds and hearts, and invite us into a discipleship that is both delightful and demanding. Send us out encouraged, enthused, and empowered, with the energy and Spirit of Pentecost, when tongues of fire descended upon your people. Amen.

OPENING PRAYER (LUKE 10)

Come, Holy Spirit, wash over us with your transforming presence. In this hour, let us know again your desire to guide, your power to teach, and your promise to heal. In our time together, give us certainty that the kingdom of God has come near. Amen. (Sherry Parker)

OPENING PRAYER (INDEPENDENCE DAY)

Lord of all nations, ruler over all time, we bow before you and give thanks for your kingdom. In the midst of our celebration of national independence, help us remember where our ultimate allegiance belongs. Help us to lift high and wave the banner of your salvation. Help us to be the light of love reaching out as fire from a sparkler on a summer evening. Lead us to join with your saints in the ultimate parade of independence from sin and death. We ask this in the name of your Son, Jesus Christ, the author of our freedom. Amen. (Sherry Parker)

PRAYER OF CONFESSION

O God of mercy and compassion, we bow our hearts and minds before you today, knowing that we have chosen to remain unchanged in the presence of your Spirit of transformation. Forgive us for every word and deed that has brought pain to the souls of our sisters and brothers. We have refused to follow the leading of your Spirit. We have refused your healing and wholeness, and we have been reluctant to be cleansed of our spiritual illnesses. Help our unbelief, and let us know the joy of returning to you in faith and renewal. Amen.

PRAYER OF DEDICATION (LUKE 10, GALATIANS 6)

O God, we know that we reap what we sow. It is our desire to sow assistance for the needy, to provide support for your church, and to ensure the proclamation of your word. Let the pledge of these gifts, and of ourselves, be the seeds that sprout evidence of your kingdom in this church and in our lives. Amen. (Sherry Parker)

BENEDICTION (GALATIANS 6)

Do not grow weary of doing good!
We go forth now to carry the burdens of one another.

To the glory of God, let us walk in the Spirit of freedom.
We go forth to live, and to offer to all,
the freedom we know in Christ.
Be changed and know the joy of new beginnings!
We go forth in joy and laughter, to serve the world,
and bring the kingdom of God to earth.

JULY 11, 2004

Sixth Sunday After Pentecost

Don Shipley

COLOR
Green

SCRIPTURE READINGS
Amos 7:7-17; Psalm 82; Colossians 1:1-14; Luke 10:25-37

THEME IDEAS
The reading from Amos exposes humanity's sinful nature and our seeming indifference to that condition. Amos used everyday items and occurrences to expose this condition, which can inspire meaningful object lessons. Psalm 82 continues the critique of culture, picking up themes of law and disorder. Judges were defending the wicked rather than protecting the oppressed. God calls for a return to justice. The Colossians, meanwhile, enjoyed a reputation for godliness. Paul knew that despite a good reputation, we all need prayer, and he prayed that God might bless the Colossians with wisdom to discern the will of God. If the will of God is to love one's neighbor, then just who is that neighbor? The reading in Luke addresses this question. Jesus makes it clear that to be neighborly is to care. Humanity has a tendency to avoid involvement, but Christ calls us to act otherwise, and to engage the world.

CALL TO WORSHIP (PSALM 82)

God calls us to judge with justice.
We will judge justly.
God calls us to show no partiality to the wicked.
We will do what is right in God's sight.
God calls us to rescue the weak and the needy.
We will deliver them from the hand of the wicked.
By living God's justice and mercy
we shall be spared the judgment of God.

CALL TO WORSHIP (LUKE 10)

O God, an Israeli dies from a sniper's bullet.
A child is assaulted by an angry father.
A mother buys drugs for herself instead of milk for her children.
An abandoned infant cries for a warm embrace.
Cries go unheard.
Needs go unanswered.
Pain goes untreated.
Touch our hearts, O Lord.
Warm our souls.
Guide our steps.
Move us to love your children,
as much as we love ourselves.

GATHERING WORDS OF REFLECTION (AMOS 7)

[Lift a pitcher and place it on the Lord's Table.]
This pitcher represents a profound lesson from God. For unless we are filled with God's Spirit, we are but empty vessels. May the Holy Spirit open our eyes, as the Lord opened Amos's eyes, that we may see even ordinary things in new ways.

CONTEMPORARY GATHERING WORDS (LUKE 10)

Who among you are wounded? Who among you need our Lord's healing touch? Be assured and comforted that our Lord will not pass you by, but will stay by your side. Feel our Lord's presence this very morning.

CONTEMPORARY GATHERING WORDS (COLOSSIANS 1)

Drink from the Spirit. Be showered by God's love. Find nourishment from God's word, and bear fruit. The Colossians were known for their kindness and goodness. Drink deeply of the Spirit, that we too may develop a vital congregation known for our righteous living.

CONTEMPORARY GATHERING WORDS (PSALM 82)

Do not walk in the darkness, but live in the light. Do not stumble around in ignorance, but walk straight in the wisdom of God. May the light of God penetrate this holy place and give us light to see the path God has set before us.

OPENING PRAYER OR PRAYER OF CONFESSION (LUKE 10)

Almighty Lord, Faithful Friend, your Word begs to be heard. It pleads for us to respond. And yet we do nothing. The pain of a wounded person is ignored. The plight of a hungry child is dismissed. Touch our hearts, O patient Healer. Compel us to respond with compassion, as you have responded to us. Heal us of our callous and cold hearts, and open our eyes and hearts to the needs around us. Dwell within us, that we may bring hope and healing to the last, the lost, and to those considered to be least around the earth. Amen.

OPENING PRAYER (PSALM 82, COLOSSIANS 1)

What is your will, O God? What plans do you have for us? We strain to hear your whispers, hoping to glean a little understanding. We examine your Word, hoping to unearth a precious verse that might shed light on your intentions. We fervently pray, eager that your will can be revealed to us. But your gentle whispers are drowned out by the hubbub of our lives. Quiet our spirits, O God, that we might discover your will. May the psalmist's plea to "rescue the weak and needy" challenge us to respond. We ask this in the name of the One who taught us to love our neighbors as ourselves. Amen.

CONFESSION (LUKE 10)

We avoid your people, O God.
We avoid the eyes of the hungry and the homeless.
We do not want to peer into the soul of the anguished heart.
We do not want to converse with an addict.
We do not want to touch the diseased.
Convict us, O God.
Expose our prejudice.
Challenge our insecurities.
And let us love our neighbors as ourselves.
Amen.

BENEDICTION (AMOS 7)

[Fish a small flashlight out of your pocket.]
This is not a very powerful flashlight, but its light illuminates the darkness. May the Holy Spirit penetrate your hearts, that God's light may shine through you and illuminate the darkness of this world.

BENEDICTION (PSALM 82)

As we put on our jackets to leave God's house, let us be aware of those who often toil and are paid abysmal wages to make garments such as these. Let us consider what we can do to ease the plight of the exploited and oppressed. May the God who brings sight to the blind and words to the mute bring love and compassion to humankind.

JULY 18, 2004

Seventh Sunday After Pentecost
Mary Boyd

COLOR
Green

SCRIPTURE READINGS
Amos 8:1-12; Psalm 52; Colossians 1:15-28; Luke 10:38-42

THEME IDEAS
Both Amos and Luke stress the importance of being still and hearing the word of the Lord. Amos, Psalm 52, and Colossians contrast life apart from God, which is filled with injustice, greed, and hostility, with life in God, which flourishes in peace, justice, and reconciliation. In a hymn of praise, Colossians describes Jesus Christ with a multitude of images, none of which fully encompasses the mystery of the Word made flesh.

CALL TO WORSHIP (AMOS 8)
Our hearts are hungry.
We seek to hear your word.
We wander from sea to sea, but we do not hear.
We run to and fro, but we do not find the word we seek.
Come to this quiet place; center your hearts.
We will hear the word of the Lord.

CALL TO WORSHIP (PSALM 52)

Like green olive trees, growing in the house of the Lord,
we flourish in God's presence.
Let us trust the steadfast love of the Lord
forever and ever.
Let us thank the Lord
forever and ever.
Let us proclaim the name of our God.
We declare God's steadfast love.

CONTEMPORARY GATHERING WORDS OR CALL TO WORSHIP (LUKE 10)

Come and worship.
But the house is a mess!
Come and worship.
But the bills need to be paid!
Come and worship.
We have too much to do!
Come and worship.
Leave the distractions behind.
Come and worship.
Sit at the feet of our Lord.

CALL TO WORSHIP (COLOSSIANS 1)

Jesus Christ is the image of the invisible God, the first-born of all creation.
All things were created through and for the Word made flesh.
Jesus is the head of the body, the church.
Jesus is the beginning, the firstborn from the dead.
In Christ, the fullness of God was pleased to dwell.
Through Christ, God is at work in the world, reconciling all things.
Come as a reconciled and holy people.
Worship Jesus Christ, our hope and glory.

PRAISE SENTENCES (PSALM 52, COLOSSIANS 1, LUKE 10)

I will trust in the steadfast love of God, forever and ever! God's name is good! Here, in the presence of the faithful, we proclaim God's name! Jesus is the image of the invisible God, through whom all things were made! In Jesus, God is reconciling all things! Listen to God's word.

OPENING PRAYER (COLOSSIANS 1, LUKE 10)

God of our busy days, God of our quiet hearts, come to us and speak your word of peace and reconciliation. Make yourself known to us, that we may be your faithful witnesses. Amen.

OPENING PRAYER (COLOSSIANS 1)

Christ Jesus, image of invisible God,
    reveal yourself to us.
Christ Jesus, in whom all things were created,
    recreate us as your servants.
Christ Jesus, head of the body, the church,
    make us one.
Christ Jesus, fullness of God,
    reconcile us to God and to one another.
Amen.

OPENING PRAYER (PSALM 52, LUKE 10)

Caring Creator, when the winds of life demand much from us, we grow weary. Away from your presence we do not flourish. Pour your word into our thirsty spirits and bring us back to life. Teach us to be faithful, fed by the abundance of your steadfast love. Amen.

PRAYER OF CONFESSION (LUKE 10, COLOSSIANS 1)

Wise and compassionate God,
    the demands of our lives keep us
    from hearing your word.

It is so easy to get lost in lists and tasks,
  to listen to what others think we should be doing.
Quiet our hearts, and open our minds,
  that we may hear you speak the true word
  of peace and reconciliation. Amen.

PRAYER OF CONFESSION

Loving God, we so often fail you.
We are so distracted by life
  that we do not pause to hear your word.
We focus on our own concerns,
  and forget the needs of others in our community.
We allow anger and hostility to grow and fester,
  choking off relationships.
We wander to and fro seeking wisdom,
  but forget that all wisdom lies in you.
Forgive us when we fail you,
  and show us a better way. Amen.

PRAYER OF CONFESSION (AMOS 8, PSALM 52)

Caring God, as the summer fruit quickly spoils, our good intentions quickly fade before the demands of life. Self-interest hardens our hearts to the cries of the poor. Little deceits grow into lives of self-delusion. Our words hurt and deceive, causing estrangement and pain. Remake us from within, O God, that we may be ever faithful to your love. Amen.

WORDS OF ASSURANCE (COLOSSIANS 1)

Jesus has reconciled you, and presents you blameless, holy, and irreproachable. Continue, securely established and steadfast in the faith.

WORDS OF ASSURANCE (PSALM 52, COLOSSIANS 1)

God's steadfast love is trustworthy. God hears our cries and forgives our sins, reconciling us in hope and peace.

PRAYER OF DEDICATION (AMOS 8, COLOSSIANS 1)

Eternal God, you have given yourself to us in Jesus Christ, the firstborn of creation. Accept these gifts we bring, and use them to care for those who are poor and needy, that the world might know justice. Use us as servants of your gospel, that we may spread the word of Jesus Christ. Amen.

BENEDICTION (AMOS 8, COLOSSIANS 1)

People are poor and oppressed and cry out for justice.
Send us forth as servants of the gospel!
People are estranged and hostile.
Send us forth as servants of the gospel!
People hunger for the word of the Lord.
Send us forth as servants of the gospel!
God commissions us for service.
Send us forth as servants of the gospel!

BENEDICTION (COLOSSIANS 1)

Go into the world as servants of the gospel,
making the word of God fully known to all people.
May the blessings of the invisible God,
the peace of Jesus Christ,
and the encouragement of the Holy Spirit
surround you now and forevermore.

BENEDICTION (COLOSSIANS 1)

Hear the holy mystery: Christ is in each of us.
Carry this mystery into the world,
sharing the good news,
so that all may know God's peace.

BENEDICTION (COLOSSIANS 1)

May the word of God, the mystery of faith, guide your life. May the presence of Christ, the fullness of God, live within you. May the Spirit of God, the hope of glory, shine through you. May you go forth with this peace and this promise.

JULY 25, 2004

Eighth Sunday After Pentecost
Melanie Carey

COLOR
Green

SCRIPTURE READINGS
Hosea 1:2-10; Psalm 85; Colossians 2:6-15 (16-19); Luke 11:1-13

THEME IDEAS
The Scriptures speak of our partnership with God in restoring God's realm, and of the promise of restoration. As the summer kicks into full gear, and many of you head out for vacation and times with nature, we are reminded of the biblical mandate to keep and restore the beauty and bounty of God's realm. A theology of ecology and God's call upon us to care for and restore creation permeates this Sunday's readings.

CALL TO WORSHIP (PSALM 85 AND LUKE 11)
The earth and its people call out for healing.
Restore us again, O God of our salvation.
The skies cry out to blow clean once again.
Restore us again, O God of our salvation.
Hallowed be your name, O God.
May your kingdom come! May your will be done, on earth as it is in heaven.

PRAISE SENTENCES (PSALM 85)

God speaks words of restoration.
God's salvation is at hand.
Faithfulness will spring up from the ground.
Righteousness will look down from the sky.
The Lord will give what is good,
    and our land will yield its increase.
Righteousness will clear the path.

PRAISE SENTENCES (HOSEA 1)

The number of God's holy ones is like the sand of the sea.
God claims them as the Lord's.
God's love continues to call us to be a holy people.

OPENING PRAYER (LUKE 11)

Lord, teach us to pray, as you would have us pray. Let us
hallow your name as we work with you to establish your
realm on earth as it is in heaven. Help us to care for all
creatures in your world, and to bring justice to those who
lack daily bread. Nourish us with your bread of life, that
we may continue to live in your love. Inspire us to serve
you in all your ways. Amen.

PRAYER

God of love, we give thanks for your promise of restoration. As we delight in the summertime earth, keep us
mindful of your creation, and our obligation to be good
stewards of all of its bounty and beauty. May we build up
your kingdom here on earth. In Christ's name we pray.
Amen.

RESPONSIVE PRAYER OF THANKSGIVING (PSALM 85)

We give thanks for the earth.
**We promise to work with God, to heal the earth and
keep it healthy.**

We give thanks for the waters—oceans, lakes, rivers, ponds, and streams.

We promise to work with God, to heal them and keep them healthy.

We give thanks for the trees, the mountains and the valleys, and all of God's creatures.

We promise to work with God, to heal the earth and keep it healthy. Thank you God for restoring your people and your earth.

BENEDICTION (COLOSSIANS 2)

Continue to live with your lives rooted in Christ.

You are built up in Jesus.

You are established in the faith.

Go forth in thanksgiving to build up God's kingdom.

Go forth in Christ's name to heal the earth.

AUGUST 1, 2004

Ninth Sunday After Pentecost
Mary J. Scifres

COLOR
Green

SCRIPTURE READINGS
Hosea 11:1-11; Psalm 107:1-9, 43; Colossians 3:1-11; Luke 12:13-21

THEME IDEAS
The scriptures of the Ordinary Season do not lend themselves to one common theme. However, common themes often emerge, as they do here. Hosea and Psalm 107 lift up the image of a God who forgives relentlessly, a God who refuses to give up on us no matter how dreadful our sins might be. Colossians and Luke, although not directly related to one another, focus our attention on the things of God's world, the mind of Christ, and the treasures of heaven.

CALL TO WORSHIP (PSALM 107)
O give thanks to the Lord.
For God is good!
God's love endures forever and ever.
God's works are wonderful!
God has saved us from our troubles.
We praise God's name!

God fills us with good things.
God satisfies our thirst with living water.
Let everyone praise the Lord.
Praise be to God!

CALL TO WORSHIP (HOSEA 11)

We are children of God—a God who loves us.
We are children of the One who taught us to walk in holy ways.
We are children of love—a love that knows no end.
We are children of the One who holds us in arms of compassion.
We are children of kindness—a kindness that binds us together.
We are children of the One who heals us in our times of trouble.
We are children of compassion—a compassion that forgives our sins.
We are children of the One who feeds us with the Bread of Life.
We are children of God—a God who loves us.

CONTEMPORARY GATHERING WORDS (PSALM 107)

Give thanks to God!
For God is good!
Give thanks to God!
For God is good!
Give thanks to God!
For God is good!

CONTEMPORARY GATHERING WORDS (PSALM 107)

God is good,
all the time!
And all the time,
God is good!

Praise Sentences (Psalm 107, Hosea 11)

Give thanks to God, for God is good!
Thanks and praise to God for Christ's amazing love!

Opening Prayer (Colossians 3)

Christ, our Life and our Love, help us to set our minds on heavenly things during this time of worship. Clothe us with your love and your compassion, that when we leave this place and continue in our earthly lives, we might bring a bit of heaven into your world. Amen.

Prayer of Confession (Hosea 11)

Mother God, too often we have been your disobedient children. When you called us, we turned away. When you taught us to walk, we ran from you. When you held us in your arms, we fought for freedom from your bonds. When you fed us with the Bread of Life, we chose food that does not satisfy. Even as we turn away from you, call us back, Father God. Be the patient parent who never gives up on us. Reach us with your compassion, that we will follow in your ways and live in your love, all the days of our lives. Amen.

Prayer of Confession (Luke 12)

Christ of compassion, help us to store your treasures in our hearts—treasures of love and kindness, compassion and justice. For investing ourselves in the lesser things of this world, forgive us. For the times when we have acted with greed and selfishness, forgive us. For the days when we have spilled over with anger and malice, forgive us. For the moments when we have shared slander and abuse, forgive us. Help us to act with charity and giving hearts. Fill us with your Spirit, that we might overflow with understanding and tenderness. Correct our tongues, that we might share words of wisdom and support. Help us, Christ Jesus, to be more like you. Amen.

BENEDICTION (COLOSSIANS 3)

Go into the world as God's children,
   forgiven and free.
Go into the world as Christ's chosen ones,
   full of love and grace.
Go into the world filled with God's Spirit.
   We go to love as God has loved us.

BENEDICTION (PSALM 107)

We have been filled with the Bread of Life, the Living
Water. Let us go forth and share the food of human compassion with all we meet. Like Living Water, let us pour
out God's love on a world thirsting for good news.

AUGUST 8, 2004

Tenth Sunday After Pentecost
Phil Harrington

COLOR
Green

SCRIPTURE READINGS
Isaiah 1:1, 10-20; Psalm 50:1-8, 22-23; Hebrews 11:1-3, 8-16; Luke 12:32-40

THEME IDEAS
We find a full range of God's emotional response to humanity in this week's scripture. Isaiah proclaims God's poetically voiced impatience with empty religious practice, while the gospel proclaims God's deep pleasure in providing the riches of the kingdom. The scriptures convey everything from, "trample my courts no more," and "I will tear you apart," to "Do not be afraid, little flock," and an invitation to meet God face-to-face, "Come now, let us argue it out." Balancing the movement between judgment and grace will be important in this service.

CALL TO WORSHIP (ISAIAH 1, LUKE 12)
God, who does not delight in empty worship, awaits our presence.
We come with open and honest hearts to hear God's word.

God, who takes pleasure in giving us the kingdom, comes to serve the faithful.
We stand with open hands to receive God's blessing and to offer God our praise.

CALL TO WORSHIP (PSALM 50)

The heavens declare God's righteousness.
The earth proclaims God's justice.
God's people gather for judgment.
The thankful are shown the way of salvation.

CONTEMPORARY GATHERING WORDS (ISAIAH 1)

God is ready to argue! Come, everyone who dares to see what the fuss is all about.

OPENING PRAYER (ISAIAH 1)

We come into your presence, O God,
pausing for self-examination,
hoping that our rebellion gives way to obedience.
Help us forsake pretentious plans to impress you
with our words, our gestures, and our offerings.
You do not desire our parroted praise,
our thoughtless singing, or our proud prayers.
You desire only that we come to you with open hearts,
and with sincerity, even in our disagreements.
You call us here. *(pause)*
We are here.

OPENING PRAYER (HEBREWS 11)

We come to you again, O God, in faith. Following the footsteps of our ancestors Abraham and Sarah, we seek assurances for our hopes and beliefs. Like them, we are strangers and aliens in this world. God, be our homeland. For in you alone, we find forgiveness for our sin, comfort for our sorrow, healing for our pain, rest for our weariness, and courage to pursue our calling. Help us now in our praise, in our meditation on your word, and in the offering of ourselves, to worthily and with integrity, call you our God.

PRAYER OF CONFESSION

God, it is easier to come to church, than it is to seek justice, rescue the oppressed, defend the orphan, and plead for the widow. We confess our faith with our lips, but not with our feet. While Abraham and Sarah walked their faith, setting out for your promised land, we have feet of clay. But we are not content to remain like this. We will choose obedience, not rebellion. We will jump into your holy waters, and we will be made clean. We will refuse complicity with evil, and we will seek your justice. Show us the way of your salvation, O God, and we will be saved. Amen.

BLESSING (LUKE 12)

May it please God to give us the kingdom;
and may we find room to receive it.

BLESSING (HEBREWS 11, LUKE 12)

As God's beloved children, receive God's blessings. As Christ's beloved disciples, receive God's blessings. As the Holy Spirit's beloved people, receive God's blessings.

DISMISSAL (HEBREWS 11)

Go now to find your homeland, your better country, the city God prepares for you.

DISMISSAL (LUKE 12)

Dressed for action, with light for our way, let us now go forth to open doors for Christ!
We will go forth, ready for the unexpected.

AUGUST 15, 2004

Eleventh Sunday After Pentecost
Lawrence A. Wik

COLOR
Green

SCRIPTURE READINGS
Isaiah 5:1-7; Psalm 80:1-2, 8-19; Hebrews 11:29–12:2; Luke 12:49-56

THEME IDEAS
Faith calls us to make choices. What will we accept? What will we reject? The gospel text challenges us to take sides. Will we accept, or reject, Jesus and his message? Jesus wants us to decide for ourselves what is right—right now! The path to peace, being strewn with division, calls for decision. The Epistle reading likewise challenges us. It calls on us to choose Jesus' life of faithful perseverance, as so many have done before us, and to aspire to God's promised joy, even amidst the harsh realities of the life of faith. The Hebrew Scripture reading contains the familiar Song of the Vineyard, after which God calls to us, "Judge [choose] between me and my vineyard" (Isaiah 5:3). We are invited to choose God and God's justice. In order to choose life, the psalm recognizes our dependence on God. While verses 3 and 7 are left out of the Revised Common Lectionary, you may want to include them. Along with verse 19, these verses form a refrain of

increased urgency: "O God," "O God of hosts," "O Lord God of hosts; let your face shine, that we may be saved."

CALL TO WORSHIP (ISAIAH 5, PSALM 80)

Beloved God, come. Clear in us a place to grow in grace.
Make of us a pleasant planting, bearing fruits of love.
Beloved God, come. Plant in us your Son, the one true Vine.
Make of us a pleasant planting, branches of your love.
Beloved God, come. Build in us a dwelling for your Spirit.
Make of us a pleasant planting, rooted in your love.

CONTEMPORARY GATHERING WORDS (HEBREWS 11)

We have come together to learn of love—
a love that witnesses to faith in Jesus.
We remain together for the sake of joy—
a joy that comes through faith in Christ.
We will go forth together, to share our hope—
a hope that lives by faith in God.

CALL TO WORSHIP (LUKE 12)

When will our hearts find peace?
Our hearts remain restless till they find their rest in God.
Did Christ come to bring peace to the earth?
Not without pain and discord, struggle and division.
Will we trust in Christ's promise: "Peace I leave with you, my peace I give to you"?
We will receive God's perfect peace, though it passes our understanding. We will accept both the promise and the challenge of peace, and choose to walk by faith.

PRAYER OF CONFESSION (PSALM 80, ISAIAH 5)

God, by your Word you formed and ordered the world, and called it good. But we have burned it with the fires of avarice, and cut it down in contempt.

Restore us, O God. Let your face shine upon us, that we might be saved.

With your hands, you tilled the ground, and cleared for us a fertile place to grow. But we have grown wild, and yielded poor fruit. Violence, like briers, is choking our land.

Restore us, O God of hosts. Let your face shine upon us, that we might be saved.

In your love, you pruned us for justice and righteousness, and tended us with care. But we have responded with indifference and hate, and caused your creation to cry out.

Restore us, O Lord God of hosts.
Let your face shine upon us, that we might be saved.

PRAYER OF THANKSGIVING (HEBREWS 11)

God of all faith, and Lord of the faithful, thank you for helping us choose the life of faith. You gave our forebears the strength to choose freedom over slavery, righteousness over injustice, peace over disobedience. Their strength has become our strength, and their hope has become our hope. Their example gives us power for perseverance, and joy for the journey. For the sake of Jesus, in whom our faith seeks perfection, may we continue to lay aside sin, cling to the cross, and glorify you in all things.

PRAYER OF INTERCESSION (LUKE 12)

The time of decision has come. Judge for yourselves what is right.

We can interpret the events of life around us, yet we are confused about matters of faith.

Fathers have turned against sons, and sons are at odds with their fathers.

Mothers are divided against their daughters, and daughters are pitted against their own mothers.

Families are torn apart. We don't know how to settle with one another.

God, help us choose to heed your living Word. May we all be brothers and sisters, one family, united in you.

PRAYER FOR ILLUMINATION

God, as we prepare to hear your word, help us to reject those barriers that keep us from truly receiving it. Free us from the arrogance that causes us to look at the faults of others, while ignoring our own. Broaden our meager understanding of justice, that our lives might be filled with your holiness. Remove every distraction, and clear our thoughts through your Spirit. We pray this in the Spirit we have found in Christ, who is our strength and joy. Amen.

PRAYER OF PRAISE

God of Tamar, Dinah, and Rahab, God of Miriam and Ruth, God of Elizabeth, and of Mary, you are the bearer of grace and truth.

We thank you for the gift of these women, and the witness they bravely shared. We thank you for the faith of our mothers, and the lives of love they dared.

God of Moses, Gideon, and Samson, God of David and Saul, God of the prophets and apostles, you are the Savior of all who call on your name.

We thank you for the gift of these brothers, and the witness they bravely shared. We thank you for the faith of our fathers, and the lives of love they dared.

God of justice, God of the vineyard, God of the fertile earth, God of fire and baptismal water, you are the God of peace and new birth.

We thank you for the gift of your presence, and the witness your Spirit has shared. We thank you for the faith of Jesus, and the life of love he dared.

BENEDICTION

Be strong, and take courage. Choose boldly a life with God, a life of enduring joy. May the grace of God, the faith of Christ, and the righteous peace of the Holy Spirit be with you now and forevermore. Amen.

BENEDICTION (ISAIAH 5)

Choose between the sinful vineyard, and our God of justice.

We choose God!

Choose between the world and its peace, and Christ whose peace demands decision.

We choose Christ!

Choose between a despairing soul, and God's enduring Spirit.

We choose God's Spirit!

Choose this day whom you will serve.

We choose to serve the Lord!

Go forth and live your choices in boldness and strength.

Amen, we say! Amen!

AUGUST 22, 2004

Twelfth Sunday After Pentecost
B. J. Beu

COLOR
Green

SCRIPTURE READINGS
Jeremiah 1:4-10; Psalm 71:1-6; Hebrews 12:18-29; Luke 13:10-17

THEME IDEAS
A theme running throughout the above scriptures is rescue. Before Jeremiah was born, God had consecrated him to be a prophet—to rescue God's people from aimlessness and sin. The psalmist seeks refuge in the God who rescues us from earthly perils. Hebrews takes this idea to a cosmic level, indicating that the whole created order will be shaken, and that Christ has come as a mediator to rescue us from all that does not endure. In Luke, Jesus rescues a woman from an infirmity she has suffered for eighteen years. In a world full of peril, rebellion, and decay, God is present to rescue us and offer us a kingdom that cannot be shaken.

CALL TO WORSHIP (PSALM 71)
O God, you are our rock and our refuge, our fortress in times of trouble.
Bless God's holy name!

You save us from the hand of the wicked, from the grasp of the unjust and the cruel.
Bless God's holy name!
We praise you, O God. From the cradle to the grave, we sing your praises.
Bless God's holy name!

CALL TO WORSHIP (HEBREWS 12)

God is shaking the earth. Where shall we stand?
We will stand on the promises of God.
God is shaking the earth. Where shall we turn for support?
We will lean on the everlasting arms of God.
God is shaking the earth. Where shall we look for our salvation?
We will look to Jesus, the mediator of a new covenant, the One who speaks the words of life.

CONTEMPORARY GATHERING WORDS (JEREMIAH 1)

Listen, God is calling.
We will listen to the Lord.
Listen, God has a Word for us to share with the world.
We will listen to the Lord.
Listen, God is calling us to be Christ's disciples.
We will listen to the Lord.

PRAISE SENTENCES (LUKE 13)

God has set us free.
Praise God!
God has made us whole.
Praise God!
Praise the Lord, your God.
Praise God!

PRAISE SENTENCES (PSALM 71)

God is our rock and our salvation.
Blessed be the Lord!

God is our fortress against the storm.
Blessed be the Lord!
God is our help in times of need.
Blessed be the Lord!

OPENING PRAYER (LUKE 13)

Great Spirit, our true healer, come to us this day. Like the
woman in the synagogue,
bent and unable to stand,
we find ourselves crippled by our demons.
Make us whole,
O God, that we may be a people of healing.
Set us free from all that binds us,
that we may break the chains of others.
Amen.

OPENING PRAYER (PSALM 71, HEBREWS 12)

God of power and might,
you are our one true refuge,
our fortress against the storm.
When the forces of evil surround us,
rescue us from the grasp of the wicked.
When the tempest enfolds us in gloom and despair,
save us from our doubts and misgivings.
Be our rock and our salvation,
that we might know your unshakable kingdom. Amen.

PRAYER OF CONFESSION (JEREMIAH 1)

Eternal God, you knew us before we were conceived in
our mothers' womb. Forgive our efforts to hide our
struggles from you. Forgive our excuses for failing to act
in accordance with your holy will. Forgive our failure to
trust that you are with us and will sustain us. We ask this
in the name of the One who calls us and equips us for
ministry. Amen.

ASSURANCE OF PARDON (JEREMIAH 1)

Just as God touched Jeremiah's mouth, giving him words to speak, God will touch our lives and make us whole. God accepts each of us as disciples of the living Christ. Follow Christ and be whole.

BENEDICTION (JEREMIAH 1, LUKE 13)

God has set us free.
  God's Spirit is upon us.
God has made us whole.
  God's Spirit moves within us.
God has called us to witness to a world in pain.
  God's Spirit sends us forth.
Go with God's blessings.

AUGUST 29, 2004

Thirteenth Sunday After Pentecost
Mary J. Scifres

COLOR
Green

SCRIPTURE READINGS
Jeremiah 2:4-13; Psalm 81:1, 10-16; Hebrews 13:1-8, 15-16; Luke 14:1, 7-14

THEME IDEAS
Two themes arise on this Ordinary Sunday, one from the Hebrew Scriptures and one from the New Testament readings. The readings from Jeremiah and Psalm 81 emphasize the importance of returning to God. These scriptures remind us of God's loving desire for us to follow God's ways. The readings from Hebrews 13 and Luke 14 emphasize the importance of welcoming and loving the stranger, the unknown, the unimportant, and the overlooked. These scriptures remind us of God's loving care for those who are marginalized by society.

CALL TO WORSHIP
Let us come into God's presence.
We come to worship the Lord.
Let us offer a sacrifice of praise to God.
We come to sing praises to God.

Let us confess God's holy name.
We come to profess God's strength and glory.
In the name of God our Creator, Redeemer, and Sustainer,
we will worship together.

CONTEMPORARY GATHERING WORDS (PSALM 81)

Sing to God.
We'll sing God's praises!
Sing to God.
We'll sing God's praises!
Sing to God.
We'll sing God's praises!

CONTEMPORARY GATHERING WORDS (PSALM 81)

Sing to God. Shout for joy!
Sing to God. Shout for joy!
Sing to God. Shout for joy!
Sing to God. Shout for joy!

PRAISE SENTENCES (PSALM 81)

God is the strength of my heart!
God is the strength of my heart!
Sing to God, our Strength, and our Redeemer!

PRAISE SENTENCES (HEBREWS 13)

God is my helper!
I shall not be afraid!
God is my helper!
I shall not be afraid!

OPENING PRAYER (LUKE 14)

Jesus, our Host, we come to your banquet table with hearts full of past events. Some of us come with regrets and misgivings. Some of us come with joy and excitement. Some of us come with pride and self-righteousness.

Turn our hearts to you, Christ Jesus, that we might be present to the gifts at your table. Humble our souls, and quiet our minds, that we might be welcome guests. Let us worship you in spirit and in truth this day. Amen.

PRAYER OF CONFESSION (JEREMIAH 2, PSALM 81)

God of Israel and Egypt, God of yesterday and today, forgive us for the times when we have wandered far from your presence. Forgive us, Gracious One, for ears that refuse to hear your voice, for hearts that refuse to follow your guidance. Help us to walk in your ways, and focus our hearts on you. Welcome us when we return, and fill us with your Living Water. Help us to know the satisfaction of being fed by your Loving Spirit. In your Holy Name, we pray. Amen.

WORDS OF ASSURANCE (PSALM 81, JEREMIAH 2)

"Return to me," says the Lord, "and I will feed you with the finest of wheat. I will draw honey from dry rocks to satisfy your hunger, and pour fountains of living water into your thirsty souls."

CLOSING PRAYER (HEBREWS 13, LUKE 14)

God of finest wheat and sweetest honey, you have filled us with good things during our time of worship. Take our full hearts, and transform them into lives that share your Word of Life with those we meet—stranger and friend, rich and poor, old and young. Let us be your instruments of loving welcome in all that we do and all that we say. Amen.

BENEDICTION (HEBREWS 13, LUKE 14)

Let mutual love continue as we leave this place.
We will share our lives and ourselves with one another.

Let the hospitality of Christ guide us as we leave this place.

We will welcome the stranger and invite the poor into our lives.

And may the love of God keep our hearts and our minds in Christ Jesus. Amen.

SEPTEMBER 5, 2004

Fourteenth Sunday After Pentecost
Brenda Tudor

COLOR
Green

SCRIPTURE READINGS
Jeremiah 18:1-11; Psalm 139:1-6, 13-18; Philemon 1-21; Luke 14:25-33

THEME IDEAS
God is able to transform everything for the good. God's love informs our choices, relationships, and decisions. The choice for God, our commitment to gospel living, brings us back to closeness with the Creator who knows us so well. The human condition is one of choice and challenge: choose obedience for goodness and salvation, or choose evil for uselessness and destruction. God's love is total and complete. God wants our full commitment. It is not by dread, demand, or duty that we live by God's ways. It is by choice, preference, and desire that we choose to do more than is required for God.

CALL TO WORSHIP
Come closer. Look here! God has called you to this place of worship.

We are here, but the burdens of the past keep us at a distance.

Forget your past. Set aside your distractions. Leave your regrets for things left undone, and come into the Lord's presence.

We are here, trying to set aside the worries that too frequently define us.

Be assured that no wound or blemish can separate us from the holy.

We are one in the Lord.

Come closer. Quiet yourself. Be refreshed and restored. You are welcome here.

We are one with the Lord. Praise God!

OPENING PRAYER

God of all blessings,
    make our worship a time of revelation.
Show us a glimpse of your realm.
Teach us how we can become what you envision.
Remind us that your love is at work in us,
    penetrating our hardness of heart.
We thank you for blessing our lives,
    showing us the joy of doing more than is required.
We are ready to be a blessing in your world. Amen.

PRAYER OF CONFESSION

Lord, we are stuck somewhere between "begun" and "done." We misunderstand your plan. We miscount the cost of discipleship. We overestimate our own determination, and find ourselves lost in our foolishness. Lord, we come before you, seeking transformation. Rework our fears and self-centered intentions, and give us courage to bear the cross. Complete what you have begun in us, dear God. By the power of your Holy Spirit, may your will be done. Amen.

OFFERING PRAYER

What we thought was ours is yours, O God. Help us to live this truth in all our relationships. We thank you for freeing us from roles and relationships that enslave and distract us from your will. Bless all that we dedicate to you this day, and make us fit vessels for your service. Amen.

CHILDREN'S MOMENT

With today's Jeremiah text, the potter's work can be work for the children. All the children could be given modeling clay to shape while the most essential part of the text is emphasized for them. Or, the leader could suggest that one child create and let the others guess what has been formed. It's best if the creation isn't so obvious that there's no need to try again, since the possibility of change, improvement, a divine makeover, is the point of the text. If the adult is doing the shaping for the children to guess, it's easy to shape a figure with arms outstretched as if to give a hug—then change it so the arms come together as if to pray.

UNISON PRAYER

Loving God, who can hide from your presence? Who else knows us or loves us so well? Keep on loving us, O God, and free us from all that keeps us from true intimacy with you, and with others. Heal our brokenness, and restore us to the wholeness for which we were intended. Through the vastness of your love, we are with you to the end. Amen.

BENEDICTION

Dear God, send us out into a hurting world. Let us go with your blessing, to be a blessing. May we bring light and life to people who do not yet know your love. Send us out with joy. Amen.

SEPTEMBER 12, 2004

Fifteenth Sunday After Pentecost
Sarah Kalish

COLOR
Green

SCRIPTURE READINGS
Jeremiah 4:11-12, 22-28; Psalm 14; 1 Timothy 1:12-17; Luke 15:1-10

THEME IDEAS
The theme for this Sunday is God's never-ending love. Although the passages from Jeremiah and Luke appear to be opposites, a closer examination reveals that the gospel passage affirms what is begun in the Jeremiah passage. The darkness and void that exists around us makes it seem as if God has passed judgment against us; the truth is that God is the shepherd that saves us. No matter what our external circumstances may be, God's love for us is eternal. The psalmist asks when the fortunes of God's people will be restored, and answers that God is constantly restoring the people of God. Being lost is another theme that emerges within the scripture readings. Jeremiah speaks of the judgment and devastation visited on the people for neglecting their God. The psalmist also speaks of being lost. Luke 15:1-10 includes two parables depicting loss: the lost sheep and the lost

coin. Both parables demonstrate God's searching hope for those who have lost their way.

CALL TO WORSHIP (JEREMIAH 4)

The mountains are quaking.
The hills are moving to and fro.
God will renew the people.
No one is left, even the
birds of the air have flown away.
God will renew the people.
The fruitful land is a desert.
The cities are laid in ruin.
God will renew the people.
The whole land shall be desolate.
Yet, there is still hope in the Lord.
God will renew the people.

CALL TO WORSHIP (LUKE 15)

The little lamb is lost. Does anyone care?
God cares, as a shepherd cares for the sheep.
How long will the shepherd search?
God's searching mercy is never ending.
What will happen when the lamb is found?
God rejoices whenever a sinner repents.
We are God's lambs. The Lord rejoices when we repent of our sins.
In repentance, and returning to God, we are found! Hallelujah!

CONTEMPORARY GATHERING WORDS (JEREMIAH 3, LUKE 15)

Have you heard the good news?
In the midst of devastation, God is there!
In the valleys of life, God is there!
In the lost pastures, God is there!
Are you lost? God is looking for you!

God is here, that you may be found!
Praise God!

OPENING PRAYER (JEREMIAH 4)

Almighty and loving God, even in the midst of what appears to be no end of devastation, we know that you will not forsake your people. As you saved the Hebrew slaves in Egypt, you will save us from our slavery to sin. We are your creation, and we know you will never abandon us, even in the deepest valleys. May our time of worship be blessed by the knowledge of your never-ending love. Amen.

PRAYER OF CONFESSION (PSALM 14)

Dear God:
We confess that there are times
    when we act as if you do not exist.
We are touched by corruption,
    and do abominable deeds.
We have gone astray,
    and blame others for our mistakes.
We forget to turn to you,
    and count on sinful ways
    to get us through life.
Restore our life in you, O God.
May each step we take cause your anointed
    to rejoice, and your people to be glad.
Amen.

RESPONSE TO THE WORD (1 TIMOTHY)

Loving God, we thank you that we have a second chance. The gift of your Son, our Savior, Jesus Christ, has enabled us to put our former ways behind us, and commit our lives to you. Use our lives as an example to others, that they too may come to know you, and commit their lives to your service. Amen.

CHILDREN'S MOMENT

Ask the children if they have ever lost something important and then found it. Get them to talk about the feelings they had. Then tell them that God feels like that when we make a commitment to believe and follow Jesus.

BENEDICTION

Let us go forth from this time of worship filled with the love of Jesus Christ. Go with hearts strengthened and renewed through the never-ending love of God. As the shepherd cares for the sheep, so too Jesus Christ looks after us. Spread this news to all you meet! Go in peace. In the name of the Father, and of the Son, and of the Holy Spirit. Amen.

SEPTEMBER 19, 2004

Sixteenth Sunday After Pentecost
Erik Alsgaard

COLOR
Green

SCRIPTURE READINGS
Jeremiah 8:18–9:1; Psalm 79:1-9; 1 Timothy 2:1-7; Luke 16:1-13

THEME IDEAS
Today's gospel lesson centers on money and materialism. The parable features a rich man, a dishonest steward, warnings about wealth and greed, and faithfulness. Jesus addressed this parable to his disciples immediately after telling several parables to the Pharisees "who were lovers of money" (v. 14). The contrast is striking: followers of Jesus are to be faithful and true to God in all things, large and small, not just the "big ticket items."

CALL TO WORSHIP (PSALM 79)
Give thanks to the Lord, for the Lord is good.
God has erased the iniquities of our ancestors.
The compassion and love of God are mighty and quick.
Deliver us, O Lord, and forgive our sins.
Why do the nations say, "Where is their God?"
Your people give thanks to you forever.

From generation to generation,
we will lift praises unto you!

CALL TO WORSHIP (1 TIMOTHY 2)

With supplications, prayers, intercessions,
and thanksgiving,
let us sing praises to God!
For kings and queens, presidents and governors,
we pray for God's blessing.
Come to the knowledge of the truth: God desires that
everyone be saved.
There is one God, and one Son, Jesus the Christ.
With songs of praises on our lips, and joy in our hearts,
let us sing praises to God!

CALL TO WORSHIP (LUKE 16)

From vain worship of worldly treasures, Jesus calls to us:
"Christian, love me more than these!"
From the idols that hold us in their sway, Jesus calls to us:
"Christian, love me more than these!"
In our joys and hours of ease, Jesus calls to us:
"Christian, love me more than these!"
In cares and pleasures, still he calls to us:
"Christian, love me more than these!"

CONTEMPORARY GATHERING WORDS
(1 TIMOTHY 2)

Enter into the presence of God with thanksgiving!
Jesus our Lord has died for us!
Enter into the presence of God with prayer.
Jesus our Lord has died for us!
Enter into the presence of God with humility.
Jesus our Lord has died for us!
Enter into the presence of God with praise!
Jesus our Lord has died for us!
A ransom for all, to bring us to truth!

PRAISE SENTENCES (1 TIMOTHY)

Christ is merciful.
Thanks be to God!
Christ offers us eternal life.
Thanks be to God!
Christ is our King.
Thanks be to God! (B. J. Beu)

PRAISE SENTENCES (LUKE 15)

Christ is our shepherd.
Praise be to God!
Christ seeks for the lost.
Praise be to God!
Christ leads us home.
Praise be to God! (B. J. Beu)

OPENING PRAYER (LUKE 16)

Gracious and loving God, you bestow blessing upon blessing upon us, your humble servants. Grant that we may be faithful stewards over every good gift, that our lives and living may always serve you. Through Jesus Christ our Lord we pray. Amen.

PRAYER OF CONFESSION

Loving God, in a land flowing with milk and honey, there are those who have nothing. Forgive us our sins of greed and pride when we have fat wallets and others have empty stomachs. Forgive us our lust for more possessions when we have three-car garages and others have no home. Forgive us our self-preoccupation, when we complain about the high cost of energy and others sleep on steam grates for warmth. Take the talents and abilities we have to earn wealth, and use them for your purposes. Enable us to share the gifts you give, freely, wonderfully, without concern for interest or payback. Forgive us those times when we grudgingly snarl:

"what's mine is mine and what's yours is yours."
Awaken within us, through the power of your grace, a
deep dancing spirit of joy, overflowing toward peace,
holiness, and love. Amen.

BENEDICTION (LUKE 16, JOSHUA 24)

You have heard the Word. "Choose this day whom you
will serve. As for me and my household, we will serve
the Lord."

BENEDICTION (LUKE 16)

[based on Fred B. Craddock's work, as quoted in The New
Interpreters Bible, *Vol. IX, "Luke, John" p. 311]*
God sends us from this place to use the gifts we are
given. With those gifts, let us give a cup of cold water,
write a note, visit a nursing home, teach a Sunday school
class, share a meal, tell a child a story, go to choir practice, and feed the neighbor's cat.

SEPTEMBER 26, 2004

Seventeenth Sunday After Pentecost
Mary J. Scifres

COLOR
Green

SCRIPTURE READINGS
Jeremiah 32:1-3*a*, 6-15; Psalm 91:1-6, 14-16; 1 Timothy 6:6-19; Luke 16:19-31

THEME IDEAS
In the readings from Psalm 91 and Jeremiah, we glimpse an image of God's promise. The Israelites have known about broken promises and the exile that results from such brokenness. Today's readings offer a return from exile, hope of new beginnings, and the promise of new life springing from the ground. The New Testament readings, on the other hand, contain serious warnings about the temptation of riches. The responsibility of sharing those riches, and turning them into works of generosity, is laid out frankly and vividly. This might be a good day to kick off the fall stewardship campaign!

CALL TO WORSHIP (PSALM 91)
Come, all of you who live in the shelter of God's love!
We call upon God's name.
Come, all of you who seek refuge from the storms of this world.

We ask for God's protection.
Come, all of you who trust in God's steadfast faithfulness.
We seek the promises of God.
Come and worship, for God's promises are true.

CALL TO WORSHIP OR BENEDICTION (1 TIMOTHY 6)

Blessed be the Lord, the King of kings.
Blessed be the Immortal One!
Blessed be the Lord, the King of kings.
Blessed be the Light and Life!
Blessed be the Lord, the King of kings.
All honor and glory belongs to Christ Jesus,
now and forevermore!

CONTEMPORARY GATHERING WORDS (PSALM 91)

I will call upon the Lord,
my refuge and my strength!
I will call upon the Lord,
my refuge and my strength!

PRAISE SENTENCES (PSALM 91)

God is the strength of my heart.
God is my protector and my shelter.
Let us call upon God's name!
Trust in the Holy One, live in Christ's love,
and know the salvation of God!

OPENING PRAYER (1 TIMOTHY 6)

O Gentle One, we pray for your presence
among us this day.
Where there is fear, let us know your comfort.
Where there is doubt, let us know your confidence.
Where there is joy, let us know your pleasure.

Where there is regret, let us know your forgiveness.
Where there is pain, let us know your compassion.
Fill this place with your Holy Spirit,
    and may this same Spirit fill our lives in this time
    of worship, and in the week ahead. Amen.

PRAYER OF CONFESSION (1 TIMOTHY 6)

God of justice and judgment, we come to you, aware of
the ways in which we are deserving of judgment. Help us
to pursue your righteousness and forsake our selfishness.
Forgive us when we store up treasures on earth and hold
back the gifts you have given us. Help us to live lives rich
in good works, full of generosity and compassion. Help
us to share all that we have and all that we are, so that we
might come into your presence without regret. Amen.

BENEDICTION (PSALM 91)

Even as we leave this place, we remain in the shelter of
the Most High.
    We will not fear the terrors of this world.
Even as we close this time of worship, we remain in the
refuge of the Holy One.
    We will not stray from God's holy presence.
Even as we live our lives, we follow in the footsteps of
Christ.
    **We will trust in God's guidance, and live in Christ's
    love.**

BENEDICTION (1 TIMOTHY 6)

Pursue what is good:
    righteousness, godliness, gentleness, faith, and love.
Endure the temptations of this world,
    fighting the good fight of faith.
Set your hearts on God's realm,
    **letting the gifts of this world become gifts for all the
    world. Amen.**

OCTOBER 3, 2004

Eighteenth Sunday After Pentecost
Rebecca Gaudino

COLOR

Green

SCRIPTURE READINGS

Lamentations 1:1-6 (11); Psalm 137; 2 Timothy 1:1-14;
Luke 17:5-10

THEME IDEAS

Our biblical writers speak of war, loss, grief, and the
desire for vengeance. They speak of suffering for the
gospel, and the daily duties of the Christian, encouraging
us to never let up. Each writer seems to wonder how we
can keep faith alive in the context of loss and uncertainty.
The answer lies in "the promise of life" and the "spirit of
power and of love and of self-discipline" (2 Timothy 1).
These gifts enable us to do what seems impossible: like
singing songs in exile about how we cannot sing songs in
exile; or calling on a tree to transplant itself into the sea;
or waiting (patiently or not) before God who has heard
our bitter laments; or finding our faith rekindled; or living faithfully, day in and day out, even without reward or
sign of success. God's power and grace work through our
tiniest bits of faith to do the impossible in our lives and
world. This Sunday is a day to face the realities of our
world, to recognize our own faltering faith in times of

devastation, and then to gather around the table for the gifts of power and love that bind all Christians together in hope before a God who counts nothing impossible!

CALL TO WORSHIP (PSALM 137, 2 TIMOTHY 1)
[Feel free to incorporate other nations and rivers]
By the rivers of Babylon,
there we sat down, and there we wept.
By the rivers of Afghanistan,
there we sat down, and there we wept.
By the rivers of the United States,
there we sat down, and there we wept.
By the rivers of Angola and Sudan and Congo,
there we sat down, and there we wept.
By the rivers of all nations—east and west, north and south,
there we sat down, and there we wept.
Look, O Lord, and see our shared sorrow.
See our shared suffering.
Come in power and love to remind us of the promise of life.
Come in power and love to help your world!

CALL TO WORSHIP (2 TIMOTHY 1)
God has saved us and called us with a holy calling.
We come to remember God's calling!
God has entrusted us with a good treasure.
We come to hear about God's gift!
God invites us to gather around the table of life.
We come to answer God's invitation!
Let us sing our praises to God who saves, calls, and invites!

CONTEMPORARY GATHERING WORDS (LAMENTATIONS 1, PSALM 137, LUKE 17)
God calls all to this holy place, and to this table today:
all who know comfort and laughter,

all who weep bitterly in the night
and have no comfort;
all who have bread aplenty,
all who groan as they search for bread;
all who have a homeland,
all who live in exile;
all who have great faith,
all who have little faith;
all who live in the east and the west,
all who live in the north and the south.
God calls all to this holy place, and to this table today.
Welcome!

OPENING PRAYER (LAMENTATIONS 1, PSALM 137, 2 TIMOTHY 1)

O God who promises Life, we come with the knowledge and experience of much that is not life-giving. Our world is at war. Too many are in exile, without homes. Too many are hungry. Our own homes are places of battle, and we hunger for peace and love. Life-Giver, come to us and to our weary world, and renew us. Remind us that we are not alone, but have brothers and sisters in faith around the world who join us in our prayers and efforts for your new life. Work your great power in all our places of death, in the name of our Savior, Christ Jesus, who abolished death, bringing life and immortality to light; and in the name of the Holy Spirit, who lives in us and makes us one in you. Amen.

OPENING PRAYER OR PRAYER OF CONFESSION (LAMENTATIONS 1, 2 TIMOTHY 1, LUKE 17)

Creator and Giver of Life, we come into your presence today, aware that much in this world is death-dealing: conflict, violence, broken relationships, poverty and hunger. Sometimes we are a part of what is deathly. And sometimes we find that our faith begins to sputter before these challenges. It's easy to despair and give up. And so we call on you today, to come to us in power and love, to heal us of our own deathly ways. Rekindle our faith, that we may not give in to the luxury of despair. Grant us your spirit of power, love, and self-discipline, that we may show others the life that you give. In the name of our Brother Jesus, who is the promise of this life, and who binds us to all, we pray. Amen.

BENEDICTION (2 TIMOTHY 1, LAMENTATIONS 1)

Go forth, assured of our holy calling through God's purpose and grace.

We go with the calling to speak and live the good news of God's promise.

Guard this treasure entrusted to you, sharing it with those who need it most.

We go with the gift of God—a spirit of power, love, and self-discipline. We go to give!

BENEDICTION (LUKE 17, LAMENTATIONS 1, PSALM 137, 2 TIMOTHY 1)

Go forth comforted, fed at God's own table, knowing that God can do the impossible through us and our faith. In our lives and in this world, we do not labor alone.

God has given us a spirit of power, love, and self-discipline.

Go forth and comfort those who are desolate, those who sit and weep, those who have no one to comfort them.

And may the grace, mercy, and peace from God, the Father and Mother, and Christ Jesus our Lord be with us all.

OCTOBER 10, 2004

Nineteenth Sunday After Pentecost
Mary J. Scifres

COLOR

Green

SCRIPTURE READINGS

Jeremiah 29:1, 4-7; Psalm 66:1-12; 2 Timothy 2:8-15; Luke 17:11-19

THEME IDEAS

God's promises bring certain responsibilities. Even people in exile are expected to "seek the welfare" of the places to which they are sent. The psalmist, who has witnessed God's amazing works, can do nothing less than sing of God's awesome deeds. The imprisoned minister of the gospel refuses to allow God's teachings, or the ministry of Christ, to be chained. The healed leper who wants to know true healing does so only after acknowledging the gift of Christ and giving gratitude to the One who heals. After receiving the promised goodness of God, we punish ourselves when we deny the steps of faith. Exile feels like hell, and the suffering of this life seems impossible to endure. The healing that we seek is only part of the wholeness that God offers. But when we participate in our ministry with Christ, our faith will make us well, and our actions will bring a wholeness that we desperately need in all of life's circumstances.

CALL TO WORSHIP (PSALM 66)

All of the earth worships God.
We have come to worship God.
All of the earth sings glory to God.
We have come to sing God's glory.
All of the earth praises God's holy name.
We have come to praise God's holy name.

CALL TO WORSHIP (LUKE 17)

God has guided us and taught us in the past week.
We return, giving thanks and praise.
Christ has healed us and comforted us in these past days.
We return, giving thanks and praise.
The Spirit has filled us and inspired us in the time since
we last gathered.
We return, giving thanks and praise.
Let us gather in worship, and give thanks and praise to
God.
**In the presence of God the Guide, Christ the Healer,
and the Holy Spirit, we come now to worship.**

CONTEMPORARY GATHERING WORDS (PSALM 66)

Sing of God's glory.
How awesome are your works, O God!
Sing of God's mercy.
How awesome are your works, O God!
Sing of God's love.
How awesome are your works, O God!

PRAISE SENTENCES (PSALM 66)

Make a joyful noise to the Lord! Sing God's praises!
Tell of God's glory! Know that our God is awesome!

PRAYER OF CONFESSION (JEREMIAH 29)

God of Exile and Return, we do not always appreciate
what you have given us. When we build our houses and

forget the homeless, forgive us. When we indulge in our abundance, instead of sharing with the poor, show us your mercy. When we revel in the despair of our enemies, instead of praying for the welfare of all your people, grant us your grace. Dwell in us, loving God, that we might approach the world with your Spirit. Return to us, that we might return to you. Guide us, that we might shelter the homeless, act with mercy toward the poor, and forgive those who hurt us. In Christ's name we pray. Amen.

WORDS OF ASSURANCE (PSALM 66)

Rejoice in our God of awesome deeds. Come and see what God has done! The One who turns the sea into dry land can surely show mercy to those who seek forgiveness. Rejoice, for God's awesome deeds include forgiveness without limits. In the name of our awesome God, we are forgiven!

WORDS OF ASSURANCE (1 TIMOTHY 2)

God's promise is true: If we die with Christ, we will also live with Christ. Even when we are faithless, God remains faithful. Let our sins die with Christ, that we might live!

We live in Christ even as our sinful selves die with Christ. Thanks be to God!

PRAYER OF THANKSGIVING (PSALM 66 AND LUKE 17)

God of mercy and goodness, we thank you for your goodness in our lives—for second chances, for your salvation, for new life, for healing and wholeness, for forgiveness and mercy, for your love and kindness. In Christ's name we pray. Amen.

BENEDICTION (JEREMIAH 29)

Go forth with God. Build houses and live in them.
Plant gardens and rejoice in the harvest.
But as you live and dwell in God's promises,
　seek the welfare of the places where you are sent.
Pray for the people of your community.
Share your wealth and abundance.
Share your homes and food.
Give, so that others may live.
Go in joy, for you are the people of God's promise!

BENEDICTION (LUKE 17)

Get up, my friends. Your faith has made you well.
We go our separate ways, to share our faith with a world in need.
Go your way, my friends. Your faith has made you well!
We go into the world, giving thanks and praise to God!

OCTOBER 17, 2004

Twentieth Sunday After Pentecost
Carla Iris

COLOR
Green

SCRIPTURE READINGS
Jeremiah 31:27-34; Psalm 119:97-104; 2 Timothy 3:14–4:5;
Luke 18:1-8

THEME IDEAS
There is a cycle of events inherent in life. There is a time
for darkness to hold sway, for bitterness in the mouth, for
teeth to be set on edge. These times are like the waning
darkness of the moon. But a time always comes when a
new light is cast, a new covenant is made, a new and
happy day dawns. The light of the moon will wax into
the glory of the full moon, serene and gleaming, and full
of hope. These are the days when God will speak to each
of us anew—each woman, man, and child.

CALL TO WORSHIP (JEREMIAH 31)
Let us gather together to worship God, a God who
speaks to each one of us.
We come to sing praises to God, our Creator.
Let us open our minds and souls to God's Holy Spirit.
**We come to proclaim the words written on our hearts
by the Spirit.**

Let us still our racing minds, that we might hear God's quiet whisper or rushing wind.
We come to listen to God.
Come, let us worship Jesus Christ, who sent us the Comforter.
We have come!

CONTEMPORARY GATHERING WORDS (JEREMIAH 31)

The goodness, mercy, and love of God are ours today.
Hear the good news!
The justice of God prevails in the hearts of those who love God.
Hear the good news!
The hope that comes from God is before us.
Hear the good news!
The law of God shall be written upon the hearts of all people.
Thanks be to God.

PRAISE SENTENCES (LUKE 18)

Rise up, you people of God.
Do not be discouraged!
Be a people of hope,
and celebrate God's Spirit within us.
Praise God, from whom all blessings flow!

OPENING PRAYER (PSALM 119)

Because I listen to the words you speak in my heart of hearts, because I still myself to hear your quiet whisper, I have more wisdom than the aged; I have more knowledge than my teachers; I surpass my enemies in understanding. Thank you for your quiet whisper. Thank you for creating me able to listen to your thoughts. Thank you for writing your wisdom on my heart. Amen.

PRAYER OF CONFESSION (2 TIMOTHY 3)

Grant us faith, eternal God, for we have known suffering and pain, injustice and unfairness. Sustain us with the power of your love, for we have known days of darkness, and nights of despair. Forgive us Lord, for we are often crushed by guilt. Help us remember all that you have taught us, for all teaching is inspired by you, O God, as we are trained in righteousness. May your love and your forgiveness surround us as we go into the world, following the paths that you have prepared for us. Amen.

BENEDICTION

Go forth, strengthened by the knowledge of your worth.
We go, knowing God loves us.
Go forth, fortified by the tenderness of God's whisper.
We go, knowing God loves us.
Go forth upon the land, secure in the knowledge of God's love.
We go, knowing God loves us.
Go forth and spread God's love to all the world.
We go, knowing God loves us.

RESPONSIVE READING (LAITY SUNDAY)

[based on fourth Epiphany Sunday readings (Jeremiah 1, Luke 4)]
You have been chosen, called by God for God's own purpose.
You can't mean me. I am not a perfect disciple. I wouldn't know what to do.
God will equip you with gifts necessary to do the work of God.
Here I am, Lord. Your will be done.
You have been chosen, called by God for God's own purpose.
You can't mean me. I'm too young. What could I say to the world?

You shall go to whom God sends you, and you shall speak whatever God commands.

Here I am, Lord. Your will be done.

You have been chosen, called by God for God's own purpose.

You can't mean me. My work's done. Retirement means passing on the responsibility.

No matter your age, with every breath you are called— called to speak about and to live out the good news.

Here I am, Lord. Your will be done. (Sherry Parker)

OCTOBER 24, 2004

Twenty-first Sunday After Pentecost
Hans Holznagel

COLOR
Green

SCRIPTURE READINGS
Joel 2:23-32; Psalm 65; 2 Timothy 4:6-8, 16-18; Luke 18:9-14

THEME IDEAS
The theme of "pouring forth" pervades the day's scripture readings: seas and rivers in Psalm 65; abundant rain and God's Spirit in Joel 2; even, metaphorically, the apostle Paul's very life, "as a libation," in 2 Timothy. With the psalmist, this is a day for rejoicing in all that God pours forth to enrich the earth and God's people. With Paul, this is also a day to feel encouraged and to endure, struggling to do good. At the center of it all is Jesus' caution, in Luke 18, to stay humble. As in many of Jesus' parables, the hero is an ordinary (or extraordinary) layperson—a tax collector! As Joel notes, God's Spirit is poured out, not just on a few people, but "on all flesh," that all may serve God.

INVOCATION OR CALL TO WORSHIP (JOEL 2, PSALM 65, 2 TIMOTHY 4)
Pour out your abundance, O God!
We thank you for the life you give.

Pour forth the rain, as you have promised,
that we may tend and cherish the earth.
Pour out your Spirit on all flesh,
that we may see visions and dream dreams.
Refresh us this day, we pray,
that we may pour out our lives in service to you.

OPENING PRAYER OR CALL TO WORSHIP

We awaken to praise you this morning, O God,
thankful that you call us all,
thankful that you bless us all.
We awaken to praise you this morning, O God,
with visions and dreams,
**mindful that you give us all, in different ways,
a message of hope to proclaim.**
Guide us, teach us, empower us, we pray.
**Equip us for ministry in your name,
and receive this day our thanks and praise.**

CONTEMPORARY GATHERING WORDS (JOEL 2, 2 TIMOTHY 4)

Come, you people of God.
Seers of visions, dreamers of dreams,
runners of races, keepers of faith,
daughters and sons, old ones and young.
Come, exalt God!
We exalt you, O God!
Let our work praise God!
Let our lives praise God!
Let us sing praise to God!
We will sing praise to God!

PRAYER OF CONFESSION (LUKE 14, PSALM 65)

Although we mean well, O God, our thanks so easily become a boast. Carried away with commitment, we compare ourselves to others. Counting our blessings, we imagine ourselves worthier than others. Working for your justice and righteousness, we fail to acknowledge others who do the same, and judge others whose gifts are different. Forgive us our transgressions, O God. Purify our hearts. Make us grateful people. And teach us to shout and sing together for joy. Amen.

BENEDICTION (2 TIMOTHY 4)

Fight the good fight. Finish the race. Keep the faith.
May God stand by you and give you strength.
To God be the glory for ever and ever. Amen.

OCTOBER 31, 2004

Twenty-second Sunday After Pentecost/Reformation Sunday

Kirsi Stjerna

COLOR
Green

SCRIPTURE READINGS
Habakkuk 1:1-4, 2:1-4; Psalm 119:137-144;
2 Thessalonians 1:1-4, 11-12; Luke 19:1-10

THEME IDEAS
Zacchaeus, a sinner, hosted the surprise guest, Christ, for supper. He reminds us of who God is to us, and how God relates and comes to us: with a surprise, in unexpected places, in the shadow of the cross, in the midst of humanity in its glory and shame. Mary's story exemplifies this: God's Son entering the world through the most human of ways, the womb. The stories of Zacchaeus and Mary tell us that people are not accepted and loved because of their merits or non-merits. Luther's major insight was that sinners are not loved because they are beautiful, perfect, and sin-free; they are beautiful and holy because they are loved by the God who sees them beautiful and holy in Christ—the "guest" linking us to the divine. Hospitality is a related theme. Like Zacchaeus, when we host a stranger, we host God in the stranger. We should

not let appearances deceive us; hospitality is a dimension
of spiritual, holy living.

CALL TO WORSHIP (PSALM 119)

God is righteous and just.
  God's justice is everlasting.
God's judgments and intentions are eternal.
  God's word is our delight.
We gather to praise our God,
  the source of life.
We gather to be touched by God,
  the life-giving holiness.
In God's promises we trust.
  In God we are made holy.

GATHERING WORDS

In a world plagued by injustice,
we embrace the source of justice.
  God is our source of justice.
We seek for understanding,
and the fulfillment of goodness.
  God makes us instruments of justice.
We bring together our hopes and fears.
We grow together in faith and grace.
  God's righteousness gives us life.
We seek God's holiness and justice.
  In God, we have our being. Praise God!

PRAISE SENTENCES (2 THESSALONIANS 1)

With abundant faith
  we give thanks to God.
With abiding love
  we sing glory to God.
With lasting grace
  we praise you God.

PRAYER OF CONFESSION AND ASSURANCE

God, in the light of your greatness, we stand small, and seldom measure up to your expectations. Knowing that your righteousness is just, graced, and life-giving, we rejoice in the very righteousness you have given to us, and of which we are a part. Amen.

RESPONSIVE PRAYER

God, our righteousness,
   hear our prayer.
We remember and trust your word.
   God, remember us.
When we are troubled and anguished,
   we ask for understanding.
When we rejoice,
   we sing to you.
With you, and in you, we want to live.
   God, our righteousness,
   hear our prayer. Amen.

PRAYER OF CONFESSION (HABAKKUK 1)

Lord, how long shall we cry for help?
Lord, when will you hear our pleas?
   We have sinned.
We have brought about death and destruction,
   for ourselves and others.
We mourn for the destruction and violence
   around us, and in us.
We come to you, Lord.
We cry for your help, comfort, and forgiveness.
Amen.

BENEDICTION

In God, we can be embodiments of divine justice, grace, and life-giving holiness. Let us live as those who have been truly made righteous by God, and let us bring righteousness, justice, and grace to the world in which we live.

BENEDICTION (2 THESSALONIANS 1)

We pray that our God will make us worthy of God's call.
Blessed is God.
We pray that God will lead our intentions, words, thoughts, and deeds.
Blessed is God's justice and grace.
We pray that the name of Jesus Christ may be glorified in us.
Through the grace of our God, and God's Son, Christ Jesus, we are blessed and made holy.

NOVEMBER 1, 2004

All Saints Day

B. J. Beu

COLOR

White

SCRIPTURE READINGS

Daniel 7:1-3, 15-18; Psalm 149; Ephesians 1:11-23; Luke 6:20-31

THEME IDEAS

All Saints Day is a perfect occasion to lift up those who have died in the faith. When loved ones die, it often seems unfair, unjust, or even cruel. Where is God in the midst of life's tragedies? The Scriptures make it clear that in the face of persecution and evil, God is with those who maintain their faith. Indeed, God's blessings extend to the meek, the poor, the hungry, and those who have been persecuted for their faith. God does not leave us comfortless, but offers us a glorious inheritance through Christ, who is seated at God's right hand in heaven (Ephesians).

CALL TO WORSHIP (PSALM 149)

Praise the Lord! Sing to the Lord a new song.
We rejoice in the Lord.
Praise God with dance.
We will make music before the Lord, our God.

God executes justice among the peoples.
God visits judgment upon the proud.
The Lord adorns the humble with victory.
Praise the Lord!

CONTEMPORARY GATHERING WORDS (DANIEL 7)

My spirit is troubled; evil is afoot.
Salvation lies in the Lord.
My spirit is troubled; nations rise against nation.
Salvation lies in the Lord.
My spirit is troubled; God's holy ones face persecution.
Salvation lies in the Lord.
Will the holy ones of the Most High receive the kingdom?
They shall possess the kingdom of God—forever and ever.

PRAISE SENTENCES (PSALM 149)

Praise the Lord!
Sing to the Lord a new song!
Dance and sing before the Lord.
Praise the Lord with drum and guitar.
Let the faithful rejoice in God's glory.
Praise the Lord!

PRAISE SENTENCES (EPHESIANS 1)

Christ gives us our true inheritance.
All praise and glory to the Son!
Christ is the author of our hope.
All praise and glory to the Son!
Christ is the good news of our salvation.
All praise and glory to the Son!
Christ is head over all things.
All praise and glory to the Son!

OPENING PRAYER (LUKE 6)

Eternal God, you turn our expectations upside down. We are taught to trust in our wealth, our status in society, and our reputation; but you teach us that these things do not lead to life. Help us to live as Christ taught us to live. Teach us to see God's blessings for the poor, for the hungry and the sorrowful, and for those persecuted for the sake of your gospel. May our lives be a blessing to those whom you bless. May our actions be a reflection of your love for all your creatures. Teach us to follow the example of the saints who have gone before us, that we may be an example to those who follow us. Amen.

OPENING PRAYER

Loving God, you surround us with a great cloud of witnesses, whose lives bear testimony to the power of godly living. Help us see in the lives of your saints, the joy of following your precepts. Keep our eyes focused on the goal of your kingdom, that we may have an inheritance that cannot be taken from us. We pray this in the name of the One who died and rose from the dead, that death would lose its sting, Jesus Christ our Lord. Amen.

PRAYER OF CONFESSION (LUKE 6)

Spirit of Truth, we confess that we read your word selectively. We love to hear words of comfort: "Blessed are you who are poor, for yours is the kingdom of heaven." But we cringe when we hear words of judgment: "But woe to you who are rich, for you have received your consolation." We confess that we are often quicker to ease the conscience of the rich, than we are to ease the plight of the poor. Forgive our failings, and strengthen our resolve, that we may speak the fullness of your truth. Amen.

ASSURANCE OF PARDON (EPHESIANS 1)

Hear the good news. In Christ, we have received an inheritance of God's redeeming love. Through the gift of the Holy Spirit, we have been sealed in God's saving love. Amen!

BENEDICTION (PSALM 149)

Go with the Lord's blessings.
We exult in God's glory.
Go with the Lord's blessings.
We rejoice in God's saving love.
Go with the Lord's blessings.
We delight in God's victory.
Go with God.

NOVEMBER 7, 2004

Twenty-third Sunday After Pentecost
B. J. Beu

COLOR
Green

SCRIPTURE READINGS
Haggai 1:15b–2:9; Psalm 145:1-5, 17-21; 2 Thessalonians 2:1-5, 13-17; Luke 20:27-38

THEME IDEAS
The Gospel and Epistle readings share an eschatological focus. Luke focuses attention on the resurrection of the dead, while 2 Thessalonians offers courage to those who wait for the end of the age, when the tribulations of our time will cease. Likewise, the Epistle reading and the Hebrew Scripture reading from Haggai share a concern for standing fast when the very fabric of existence is shaken. The prophet Haggai exhorts the people to renew their faith in God and to commit themselves to rebuilding God's holy temple. In similar fashion, the apostle Paul exhorts the church in Thessalonica to keep the faith in the face of writings and murmurings that have shaken their fledgling faith. The psalter calls the people to praise God's holy name and to rejoice in God's wondrous works.

CALL TO WORSHIP (PSALM 145)

Our God and King, holy is your name.
You are greatly to be praised!
How wondrous are your works, O God.
You are greatly to be praised!
You fulfill the desires of all who seek you.
You are greatly to be praised!
Our God and King, holy is your name.

CALL TO WORSHIP (HAGGAI 1)

Take courage, people of God.
Throw off doubt and fear.
Even in the midst of loss?
Take courage, people of God.
Prepare your hearts for joy.
Even in the midst of sorrow?
God will shake the earth once more,
and fill this house with splendor.
Praise be to God!
God will shake the heavens once more,
and fill our lives with hope.
Praise be to God!

CONTEMPORARY GATHERING WORDS (2 THESSALONIANS 2)

Do not be afraid, for God is near.
Whom shall we fear?
Do not be afraid, salvation is at hand.
What is there to dread?
Come and be sanctified in the Lord.
In Christ, we find comfort and hope.

PRAISE SENTENCES (PSALM 145)

Great is the Lord, and greatly to be praised.
Sing God's praises!
Great is the Lord, and wondrous are God's works.

Sing God's praises!
Great is the Lord, and holy is God's name.
Sing God's praises!

PRAISE SENTENCES (HAGGAI 1)

Shake the heavens; rattle the earth.
Shout praises to our Lord!
Shake the heavens; rattle the earth.
Shout praises to our King!
Shake the heavens; rattle the earth.
Shout praises to our God!

OPENING PRAYER (LUKE 20)

Holy God, Caretaker of your people, we come to you with questions for which there seem to be no answers. We come to you with doubts that will not go away. Ease our troubled minds, that we may proclaim your truth with confidence. Unburden our hearts, that we may offer our love freely to all those we meet. Amen.

OPENING PRAYER (PSALM 145)

God of justice and truth, you are near to all those who call on you. You hear the cries of your people, and save them with your mighty arm. Help us to sing your praises, and declare the wonder of your handiwork. Embolden us to extol you all the days of our lives, that our children, and our children's children, may know of your glory. Amen.

PRAYER OF CONFESSION (2 THESSALONIANS 2)

Eternal God, your truth is as constant as the North Star, your precepts as solid as polished granite. We confess that our faith is too easily shaken. Our minds are too easily alarmed. Our feet are too quickly led down the path of rebellion. Help us distinguish your truth from the voices that would deceive us. Sanctify us with your Holy

Spirit, that the fruits of salvation may grow within us. We ask this in the name of Christ Jesus, who was and is and is to come, our glory and our light. Amen.

WORDS OF ASSURANCE (2 THESSALONIANS 2)
Hold fast to the good news of God's Word. Through the Holy Spirit, God gives us grace and power to obtain the glory of our Lord Jesus Christ. In Christ, our sins are forgiven. Amen.

BENEDICTION (2 THESSALONIANS 2)
May the Lord Jesus Christ, and our God in heaven who loves us, and gives us eternal comfort and hope, comfort our hearts and fit us for every good work.

NOVEMBER 14, 2004

Twenty-fourth Sunday After Pentecost
Joanne Carlson Brown

COLOR
Green

SCRIPTURE READINGS
Isaiah 65:17-25; Isaiah 12; 2 Thessalonians 3:6-13; Luke 21:5-19

THEME IDEAS
In times of stress, hardships, and fear, it is natural for people to turn to God for comfort and hope. The Isaiah and Luke passages appear to have very different visions. In contrast to the vision of peace and harmony in Isaiah, Luke has wars, and rumors of wars and persecutions. But in all the passages, there is a promise of deliverance. Those who dare to live out Jesus' call for justice, love, and faithfulness will see, with joy and thanksgiving, the new heaven and the new earth. This is a Sunday that can speak to the very real fears and anxieties of our times, and lift up the vision and promise of life and peace, and freedom and comfort, for the people God has claimed as God's own.

CALL TO WORSHIP (ISAIAH 12, ISAIAH 65)
Rejoice, people of God.
God is creating a new heaven and a new earth.

God delights in God's people.
God blesses the people with life and prosperity.
God hears and answers the cries of God's people.
God is our salvation.
Sing praises to God, who has done marvelous things for us.
We sing and shout for joy.

CONTEMPORARY GATHERING WORDS

God calls us to faithfulness.
We respond with joy.
God will never abandon us.
We trust in the promises of God.
God calls us to a new heaven and a new earth.
Let us journey together, with thanksgiving and praise.

PRAISE SENTENCES (ISAIAH 12)

We will give thanks to God, who is our salvation. God is our strength, we will not be afraid. Give thanks and praise to God. Shout aloud and sing for joy, for God has done marvelous things for all the people.

PRAISE SENTENCES (ISAIAH 65)

Be glad, and rejoice forever, in what I am creating: a new heaven and a new earth! God's promises are sure. They shall not hurt or destroy on all God's holy mountain! Thanks be to God!

OPENING PRAYER

God of promise and hope, be with us today. Break through our fear and anxiety with a vision of comfort and peace. Be with us, as we journey toward the new heaven and earth, that we may be a sign of your love and justice and promise to all people. Amen.

OPENING PRAYER

Faithful and life-giving God, we come with hearts full of joy and thanksgiving, for your steadfast love is with us. Be present with us in this time of worship. Walk with us, as we strive to live a life of faithfulness, ever keeping the vision of the new heaven and new earth before us. Amen.

PRAYER OF CONFESSION

God of things past, things present, and things to come, we come this morning acknowledging that we have let fear and anxiety take hold of our hearts and minds. We have not trusted your promises. We have not believed there can be a time when violence and injustice will cease. Help us to claim our citizenship in your new heaven and new earth. Help us to proclaim, to all people, your message of salvation and hope, comfort and peace. Amen.

WORDS OF ASSURANCE

God loves us with a deep and abiding love. God's promises are sure. They shall not hurt or destroy on all God's holy mountains.

BENEDICTION

Let us go forth, praising and thanking God for promises and visions, for hope and strength. Let us set out on our journey toward the new heaven and the new earth, confident that Christ walks with us every step of the way. With the help of the Holy Spirit, may we remain faithful to the vision. Amen.

NOVEMBER 21, 2004

Christc the King Sunday
Mary J. Scifres

COLOR
Green

SCRIPTURE READINGS
Jeremiah 23:1-6; Luke 1:68-79; Colossians 1:11-20; Luke 23:33-43

THEME IDEAS
The scripture readings for Christ the King Sunday focus on the themes of rescue and light. Those responsible for shepherding God's people have failed in their duties. This failure is so complete that the shepherds have actually scattered the sheep and destroyed the flock. God promises to save a remnant of the flock and raise up a righteous king who will lead wisely, and will execute justice and righteousness in the land. Christians proclaim Jesus as the righteous branch promised in Jeremiah, and the prophet of the Most High witnessed to in Luke. Christ is our true King, the Good Shepherd who leads God's flock to fullness of life.

CALL TO WORSHIP (JEREMIAH 23, LUKE 23)
God promised a king.
Christ came as a child.

God pledged to bring justice.
Christ died on the cross.
Yet, Christ is our king.
Justice comes through the grace of the cross.
Come, let us worship the God of justice and righteousness.
Come, we will worship the Christ of mercy and love.

CALL TO WORSHIP (LUKE 1, COLOSSIANS 1)

Look, the dawn has come to brighten this day.
We look for the dawn, but see only darkness.
Look, Christ has come to bring light for our darkness.
We look for Christ, but see so many sins.
Listen, Christ is more powerful than even death itself.
We listen for Christ's life, but know so much death.
Listen, Christ will guide us in God's way of peace.
We listen for God's peace, but sense turmoil and war.
Think now of Christ, God's image, the promise of the ages.
We think upon God, but our minds often wander.
Come to this place, a reminder of God's presence.
We come to worship and to find God's peace.
Come, my friends, all things are ready.
We come to this time. Let us look for God's light.

CONTEMPORARY GATHERING WORDS (JEREMIAH 23, LUKE 1)

God promised a King, a Light for our darkness.
Blessed be the Lord!
God sent Christ to earth, a Savior to guide us.
Blessed be the Lord!
God calls us to worship, as people of the promise.
Blessed be the Lord!

PRAISE SENTENCES (PSALMS, COLOSSIANS 1)

Blessed be God, who looks upon us with joy! Blessed be
Christ, who brings us new life! Blessed be the Lord!

OPENING PRAYER (LUKE 1, CHRIST THE KING)

Christ our King, come to us this day. Help us to know you as the visible God, the one who walked this earth and died as we will someday die. Help us to sense your presence, not just as a heavenly king, but as an earthly companion. Walk with us during this time of worship and in the days ahead. As we prepare for the seasons of Advent and Christmas, guide us in your ways. Lead us on the paths of peace. Light our journeys of darkness that we may know without a doubt that we are not alone. Amen.

OPENING PRAYER (COLOSSIANS 1)

Immortal, invisible God, we pray for your strength in our lives. Prepare us to endure the struggles of this life with patience and joy and thanksgiving. Show us the power of forgiveness and reconciliation. Holy God, shine through our lives in all your fullness, that others may see in our patience and joy, your glory and your strength. Fill us with your acceptance, that we may be accepting of others. Be present with us in this time of worship, strengthening and preparing us for your ministries on this earth. Amen.

PRAYER OF CONFESSION (LUKE 1)

Reconciling God, you know the times when we do not offer forgiveness as readily as we seek it for ourselves. You see us when we turn to the darkness, avoiding Christ's light. You feel the turmoil when we choose violence over peace. Forgive us, Holy One. Guide us in your ways. When we withhold forgiveness, grant us the grace to think again and extend the hand of reconciliation. When we walk in the darkness, send light for our path. When we can't find the way into peace, overwhelm us with your love. Help us to become your people, again and again. Amen.

November 21, 2004

WORDS OF ASSURANCE (LUKE 23)
Jesus remembers us, even in our sinfulness.
Truly, I tell you, we will be with Christ in Paradise.

BENEDICTION (LUKE 1, COLOSSIANS 1)
Be strong in the strength of God's power.
Prepare yourselves with patience and joy.
Give thanks to God, remembering Christ's gift.
Go with Christ's light, walking in the ways of peace.

NOVEMBER 25, 2004

Thanksgiving Day
Mary J. Scifres

COLOR
Green

SCRIPTURE READINGS
Deuteronomy 26:1-11; Psalm 100; Philippians 4:4-9; John 6:25-35

THEME IDEAS
The thanksgiving theme provided by the Revised Common Lectionary readings is always coupled with a theme of God's sustenance. God provides all that we need, and only asks for our thanksgiving and gratitude in return. This year's readings also carry a secondary theme of joy and rejoicing. As you plan your service of worship, you may want to find ways for people to weave their attitudes of giving with attitudes of joyful thanksgiving.

CALL TO WORSHIP (PSALM 100)
Come into God's gates with hearts full of thanksgiving.
  We enter God's courts with songs of praise.
Worship God with gladness and gratitude.
  We bless God's holy name, for God has given us a love that never ends.

CONTEMPORARY GATHERING WORDS (PSALM 100)

Come into God's presence with singing.
We'll sing to the Lord!
Come into God's presence with joy.
We'll sing to the Lord!
Come into God's presence with thanks and praise.
We'll sing to the Lord!

PRAISE SENTENCES (PSALM 100, PHILIPPIANS 4)

Rejoice in God always. Say with me, "We rejoice!"
We rejoice!
Bring your joyful noise to God. Worship with gladness in your hearts! Enter God's gates with songs of thanksgiving and praise.

OPENING PRAYER (JOHN 6)

Bread of Life, we come into your presence with hunger in our hearts and thirst in our souls. Fill us with your love and your light. We give thanks this day for your gracious gift of self, for filling us with your very being. With all that we have, and all that we are, we give you thanks and praise as we worship you. Amen.

OPENING PRAYER (PHILIPPIANS 4)

Prince of Peace, we ask for your presence in our worship this morning. Quiet our minds, that we may hear only what is good and true, honorable and just, worthy and pleasing to you. Focus our lives, that we may act only in goodness and truth, with honor and justice. Guide us in all that we say, and all that we do, that our worship, our ministries, and our very lives might be pleasing to you. Amen.

PRAYER OF CONFESSION (DEUTERONOMY 26, PHILIPPIANS 4)

We confess to you, Gracious God, that we have worried too much this past week. We have not always focused on the good things of this world, but rather on the troubles and turmoil that surround us. You offer us sustenance and survival, yet we long for luxury and abundance. You give us gifts of overflowing generosity, yet we squander your gifts, and act as if we lack the gifts we need to make a difference in the world. Forgive us, Loving God. Help us to turn our concerns over to you, that we might know your peace. Help us to trust in your provisions when we fear for our survival. Help us to accept your gifts with gratitude and praise. And remind us to share your abundance with others. Amen.

WORDS OF ASSURANCE (JOHN 6:35)

Jesus is our Bread of Life. Hear his words of promise and assurance: "Whoever comes to me will never be hungry, and whoever believes in me will never be thirsty." All who come to the Bread of Life are forgiven and filled. Christ's abundance makes us whole.

PRAYER OF THANKSGIVING (DEUTERONOMY 26)

God of the ages, we thank you for creating us, and molding us to be your people. For saving us in times of trouble, we give you praise. For fulfilling your every promise, we give you thanks. Since ancient times, you have walked alongside us, guided our ways, and loved us relentlessly. We are grateful for all that you have done, and for all that you are doing. Accept our thanks and praise, Generous Giver of Life. Turn our gratitude into acts of justice and mercy. Take the gifts that we return to you, and bless them to become abundant gifts for a world in need. In your loving name, we pray. Amen.

BENEDICTION (PHILIPPIANS 4)

Rejoice in God, now and forevermore.

We rejoice in our God, who hears and answers our prayers.

Take no worry for today or tomorrow.

May we think on all that is good and true, honorable and just.

Persist in all that we have learned and received from Christ.

May we know the peace of God, which passes all understanding.

Go in that peace, so that your hearts and your minds may rest in Christ Jesus.

Amen.

BENEDICTION (JOHN 6)

We have come to the well,

and been filled with Living Water.

We have worshiped the Bread of Life,

and have eaten to our hearts' content.

Go in peace, for your faith has made you well.

Go in peace, for your faith has made you well!

NOVEMBER 28, 2004

First Sunday of Advent

B. J. Beu

COLOR
Purple or Blue

SCRIPTURE READINGS
Isaiah 2:1-5; Psalm 122; Romans 13:11-14; Matthew 24:36-44

THEME IDEAS
Today marks the beginning of Advent, the time when we look to God for our promised salvation. The readings from Isaiah and the Psalms speak of that glorious time when all the peoples of the world will come to Jerusalem and worship the Lord. This will be a time of peace—a time when the nations will beat their swords into plowshares, and their spears into pruning hooks (Isaiah 2:4). The readings from Romans and Matthew speak of our need to be vigilant as we wait for the Lord's return. Salvation is nearer to us than when we first began to believe, so be vigilant. The Lord will come as a thief in the night and catch many unaware. Advent is a time of joyful preparation—a time to prepare our hearts anew to receive our Lord and Savior.

CALL TO WORSHIP (ISAIAH 2)
Come; let us go up to the mountain of God.
Prepare the way of the Lord!

Come; let us hear the word of God.
Prepare the way of the Lord!
Come; let us walk in the light of God.
Prepare the way of the Lord!

CALL TO WORSHIP (ROMANS 13)
The time has come.
The time is now.
Wake from sleep.
Come to worship!
Lay aside darkness.
Walk in the light!
Live in Christ Jesus.
Love in the Lord.
The time has come.
The time is now.
Wake from sleep.
We come to worship!

CONTEMPORARY GATHERING WORDS (MATTHEW 24)
Wait for the Lord.
Christ is coming!
Keep awake.
Christ is coming!
Be ready for God.
Christ is coming!
Prepare the way.
Christ is coming!

PRAISE SENTENCES (ROMANS 13)
The night is far gone! Day is near!
Salvation is at hand! Bless God's holy name!

PRAISE SENTENCES (ISAIAH 2)
Salvation is at hand.
Lift God's name on high!

Salvation has come to us.
Sing God's praises!
Salvation lights our path.
Worship the God of light!

OPENING PRAYER (ISAIAH 2)

Holy God, your majesty is greater than the highest mountain, your glory more radiant than the summer sun. As the days grow darker, and the earth seems barren, help us walk in your light. As the days grow colder, and nation rises up against nation, warm our hearts with your love. Strengthen our hope, and heal our broken world, that we will have the courage to beat our swords into plowshares. We ask this in the name of the One who is the Prince of Peace. Amen.

OPENING PRAYER (MATTHEW 24)

God of flood and storm,
God of sunshine and rainbow,
    you visit the earth like a thief in the night,
    catching your people unaware.
Grant that we might be found waiting,
    when you come in your glory.
Aid our vigilance,
    that we may not be swept away,
    when the time of judgment is at hand.
Cleanse us from our sin,
    that we may be fit to enter into Christ's glory.
Amen.

OPENING PRAYER OR PRAYER OF CONFESSION (ROMANS 13)

Eternal God, you offer us your salvation, a gift beyond price. We know that the night is far gone, the day is near. Yet we cannot seem to awaken. Our eyelids have grown heavy, the light hurts our eyes. Forgive our reluctance to heed your summons. Call to us once again, that we may hear your voice and follow you anew. Amen.

ASSURANCE OF PARDON (ROMANS 13)

Hear the good news. Salvation is nearer to us now than when we first believed. The One who came as a child long ago, will come again. The Holy One will reawaken our hearts, and lead us into God's eternal glory. Praise God!

BENEDICTION (2 THESSALONIANS 2)

May God grant us peace. May God establish us in righteousness. May God bless us with prosperity in every good deed. Amen.

DECEMBER 5, 2004

Second Sunday of Advent
Mary J. Scifres

COLOR
Purple or Blue

SCRIPTURE READINGS
Isaiah 11:1-10; Psalms 72:1-7, 18-19; Romans 15:4-13; Matthew 3:1-12

THEME IDEAS
The message of preparation is one that most people need to hear in early December. The time has come to prepare for Christ's arrival, and to prepare for God's realm to come to fruition. The question, "How do we prepare?" becomes increasingly pressing when we realize that most of our preparations in December are focused on decorations, purchases, gifts, and parties. To prepare for Christ's arrival, as Isaiah and John the Baptist warn, is to turn our hearts back to God, and to once again focus our lives on justice and righteousness. The day's readings can help people reclaim some sanity by remembering that Advent is our time to prepare to be Christlike in our lives, to become loving animals in the peaceable kingdom, rather than party animals in the flurry of holiday activities.

CALL TO WORSHIP (MATTHEW 3, PSALM 72)

Prepare the way of the Lord!
How shall we straighten out our lives?
Prepare the way of the Lord!
How shall we bear fruit in these barren days?
Prepare the way of the Lord!
How shall we be worthy of our Christian baptism?
Prepare the way of the Lord!
How shall we prepare the way of the Lord?
Love justice, seek mercy, walk humbly with God.
We will prepare the way of the Lord!

CALL TO WORSHIP (ROMANS 15)

Welcome, one and all, in the name of Christ Jesus!
We come to worship God, singing praises to Christ's holy name.
Welcome, Christ Jesus, in this place we call your home.
We come into Christ's presence, rejoicing this day.

CONTEMPORARY GATHERING WORDS (ROMANS 15)

Praise the Lord, all of God's people! Sing praises to God's name!
Sing praises to God's name!
Praise the Lord, all of God's people! Sing praises to God's name!
Sing praises to God's name!
Let us praise the Lord!

CONTEMPORARY GATHERING WORDS (PSALM 72)

Blessed be the Lord.
Bless God's holy name!
Blessed be the Lord.
Bless God's holy name!

Blessed be the Lord.
Bless God's holy name!

OPENING SENTENCES (ROMANS 15)

May the God of steadfastness and encouragement grant you to live in harmony with one another, in accordance with Christ Jesus, so that together you may, with one voice, glorify the God and Father of our Lord Jesus Christ. Let us worship God together!

OPENING PRAYER (ADVENT)

Loving God, bring us hope and joy on this day. Help us to prepare for the celebration of your birth on this earth. Help us to prepare for the coming of your justice and righteousness into our world. Help us to live as your people in this hour, and in the days ahead. Amen.

PRAYER OF CONFESSION (MATTHEW 3)

In this season of Advent, we pray for hearts that are truly turned to you, O Holy One. Forgive us, when we are so busy preparing our own way, that we forget to prepare for you. Help us to turn back to you, O Gracious One, that we might be truly prepared for your arrival on Christmas Day. Amen.

WORDS OF ASSURANCE (ROMANS 15)

The root of Jesse is amongst us. Christ Jesus comes to bring us hope, the long-promised hope of God.

RESPONSIVE READING (ISAIAH 11)

God promises to us a Savior.
Come, Lord Jesus.
The Spirit of God shall fill our Savior with wisdom and understanding.
Come, Lord Jesus.

The Spirit of God shall fill our Savior with counsel and might.
Come, Lord Jesus.
The Spirit of God will fill our Savior with knowledge and love.
Come, Lord Jesus.
Our Savior will not judge by what is seen or heard, but with righteousness and justice.
Come, Lord Jesus.

BENEDICTION (ROMANS 15)

May the God of hope fill you with all joy and peace in believing, that you may abound in hope by the power of the Holy Spirit.

BENEDICTION (ROMANS 15)

May the God of hope fill us with so much joy and peace, through our faith in Christ Jesus, that we may be overflowing with the hope of the Holy Spirit!

DECEMBER 12, 2004

Third Sunday of Advent
Mary J. Scifres

COLOR
Purple or Blue

SCRIPTURE READINGS
Isaiah 35:1-10; Luke 1:47-55; James 5:7-10; Matthew 11:2-11

THEME IDEAS
The above readings are an interesting mix of Advent texts, with at least one common theme: Christ will come, but it may be awhile. Even when we endure and observe suffering, we are called to believe that God's promises will be fulfilled. In spite of her young age and her difficult circumstances, Mary sings this message with complete confidence (Luke 1:47-55). James, who had waited a long time to see Jesus' teachings fulfilled, calls for patience and perseverance. Isaiah prophesied of hope and growth, even when he knew desolation and despair. Advent is a time to remember such faith, and to trust God's promises.

CALL TO WORSHIP (ISAIAH 35)
Come onto the highway of Christ,
a holy way in the wilderness of life.
Come into the presence of joy,
a place of glory and majesty.

Return to God's love,
where we shall know no fear.
Come with hearts full of song,
for sorrow and sighing have fled.
Here and now, we will find joy and gladness!

CALL TO WORSHIP (LUKE 1, ADVENT)

Come, magnify the Lord!
We come to rejoice in God's presence among us.
Come, live in the Lord.
We come to strengthen God's presence in our world.
Come, bless God's holy name.
We come to give honor and glory to the Holy One.
O come, let us adore Christ as we worship this day.

CONTEMPORARY GATHERING WORDS (ISAIAH 35)

Rejoice with joy and singing.
We come rejoicing!
Rejoice with joy and singing.
We come rejoicing!
Rejoice with joy and singing.
We come rejoicing!

PRAISE SENTENCES (ADVENT)

Christ is coming.
Christ is coming soon!
Christ is coming.
Christ is coming soon!

RESPONSIVE READING (LUKE 1)

My soul magnifies the God of Love.
My spirit rejoices in God, our Savior.
The Mighty One looks kindly on us,
and does great things for us.

God's mercy is shown from generation to generation,
   and God's strength brings justice to all.
Surely mercy and goodness shall follow us
   **all the days of our lives. And we will know the help
   and love of the Holy One, forever and ever. Amen.**

PRAYER OF CONFESSION (JAMES 5)

God of patience and perseverance,
   forgive us our impatience.
Help us to trust in your promises,
   even when the world's promises betray us.
Help us to know your patience,
   even when love and justice seem so slow in coming.
Help us to know your strength,
   even when our hearts feel weak.
Help us to know your perseverance,
   even when our work seems fruitless.
Forgive us our doubts.
Plant seeds of faith and hope in our hearts,
   that we may be patient until you arrive,
   and your realm abides on earth.
In the name of Christ who is with us even now, we pray.
Amen.

WORDS OF ASSURANCE (JAMES 5)

Be patient, beloved ones. For Christ has died. Christ has
risen. And Christ will come again!

PRAYER (ADVENT)

As the days darken and the winter winds blow, help us,
O Promised One, to keep you in our vision. Let us not
lose sight of the promise you bring in this season. Let
your light shine in the darkness for all to see. Shine
through us with your promise. Live through us with
your strength. And love through us with your mercy, that
we might be messengers of your good news. Amen.

BENEDICTION (MATTHEW 11)

Go and tell others what you hear and see.
   The blind receive sight, and the lame walk!
Go and tell others the good news of hope.
   The deaf hear and the dead are raised!
Go and tell others the promise of God's kingdom.
   The poor will know justice, and God's love will reign!
Proclaim the good news.
   There is new life in Christ!

DECEMBER 19, 2004

Fourth Sunday of Advent

Sherry Parker

COLOR
Purple or Blue

SCRIPTURE READINGS
Isaiah 7:10-16; Psalm 80:1-7, 17-19; Romans 1:1-7; Matthew 1:18-25

THEME IDEAS
In the scripture readings on this Sunday before Christmas, prophetic signs and Joseph's dream herald the coming of the Messiah. Isaiah announces the signs of the Savior, and the apostle Paul verifies the truth spoken by the prophets. The psalmist longs for the One who will be the shepherd—the One who will be the light of the world. In the Gospel text, the birth narrative unfolds by way of a dream. Emmanuel will come. Emmanuel has come. While prophetic expression often comes to us in elaborate words and startling images, God also speaks in the quiet of the night, in the simplest of dreams.

CALL TO WORSHIP (PSALM 80, ISAIAH 7, MATTHEW 1)
The reign of God is near.
Show us our shepherd, our shining light, the One who will restore all that is broken.

This shall be a sign to you. A young woman shall bear a child, and he shall be called Jesus.

Jesus is the sign and promise of our salvation.

He is Emmanuel, God with us.

Jesus is our salvation.

Come, let us worship. God is near.

Come, let us worship, Emmanuel.

GATHERING WORDS (ISAIAH 7, MATTHEW 1, ROMANS 1)

God has spoken through the prophets of old, and through the dreams and visions of the faithful. The world's delight and salvation has come in the gift of God's Son. May the grace and peace of our Lord, Jesus Christ, be with us as we gather for worship.

GATHERING WORDS (MATTHEW 1)

Joseph has a dream, and God makes way for the light of the world. Joseph and Mary give their trust, and God restores a broken people. A child is born, and the world will never be the same. Together let us watch and wait. Jesus is coming!

CONTEMPORARY GATHERING WORDS (MATTHEW 1)

At Christmas, many dream of snow, festive evergreens, and brightly wrapped packages. Joseph and Mary dreamed of a child who would save us from our sins.

Let this Child be our Christmas dream.

At Christmas, many hope for delightful gifts, and the embrace of loved ones. Joseph and Mary hoped to behold the Messiah, Emmanuel, God with us.

Let Emmanuel be our Christmas hope.

At Christmas, many look forward to services of worship with beloved hymns, and the light of candles. Joseph and Mary worshiped God, by trusting in the Word of God.

Let our Christmas worship embody our trust in God's Word, come to earth in Jesus Christ.

CONTEMPORARY GATHERING WORDS (MATTHEW 1)

Joseph	I have had a dream!
People	**What is your dream, Joseph?**
Joseph	I have heard the Lord speak.
People	**Give us a word from the Lord.**
Joseph	Mary will be my wife, and the child she carries shall be called Jesus.
People	**There is much to fear in your decision.**
Joseph	This is the work of the Holy Spirit. I will not be afraid.
People	**Mary will bear a son who will save us from our sins.**

PRAISE SENTENCES (PSALM, MATTHEW, CHRISTMAS)

God is with us!
    Glory to God in the highest!
Emmanuel, the Promised One, has come.
    Glory to God in the highest!
God's light has shined.
    Glory to God in the highest!

OPENING PRAYER (MATTHEW 1)

O God, by your Holy Spirit, we ask that you conceive in us a yearning to walk in the ways of Christ. May the commitment to compassion and mercy grow within us. Birth in us the desire for your Word and for you Way. Amen.

OPENING PRAYER (ISAIAH 7, PSALM 80)

Restore us, O Spirit of God,
    in this time of worship.
Feed us by your word.

Strengthen us in prayer.
Lead us in songs of praise.
And move us ever closer
  to the certainty that God is with us.
All praise to Emmanuel,
  our hope and our salvation. Amen.

UNISON PRAYER (MATTHEW 1)

God, Creator and Lover of this world, like the shepherds in the hills overlooking Bethlehem, you watch over us. Like the star that rose above the city of Jesus' birth, you are a beacon of light, shining in our troubled world. Like the whispered words of Joseph's dream, you give us direction and hope. God of all good gifts, strengthen us for obedience and steadfast faith. Lead us to accept your salvation in Jesus, to follow the light, and to rely on the voice of your Spirit. God of light and hope, to you be all glory, now and forever. Amen.

PRAYER OF CONFESSION (PSALM 80, MATTHEW 1)

O God, as the celebration of Christmas approaches, we struggle to remain focused on the birth of your Son. Our hope lies in your promise of redemption and restoration, yet we are easily distracted. Forgive our preoccupation with appearances, and restore us to faithful living. Forgive our selfish behavior, and restore us to compassionate living. Forgive us for ignoring your voice, and restore us to attentive prayer. Forgive us for our focus on worldly gifts, and restore our sense of awe in the gift of your Son. We give you thanks for your saving love, and for the mercy we have received in Jesus Christ. Amen.

WORD OF ASSURANCE (PSALM 27)

Wait for the Lord. Be strong, and let your heart take courage. We shall see God's goodness. Wait for the Lord!

ADVENT LITANY (ISAIAH 7, PSALM 80, ROMANS 1)

Isaiah declared that salvation would come in the birth of a child.
O come, O come, Emmanuel!
We await restoration, the drying of our tears, the renewing of our hopes.
O come, O come, Emmanuel!
We are broken in our struggle with sin.
O come, O come, Emmanuel!
We, who walk in darkness, seek the light that is coming into the world.
O come, O come, Emmanuel!
Stir up your might, O God, and save your people!
O come, O come, Emmanuel!

BENEDICTION (MATTHEW 1)

A young woman shall bear a child who will save all people from their sins.
We go forth to await the child of promise.
Spread the good news! God is with us. God will save.
We will spread the good news of Emmanuel, God with us.

BENEDICTION (ROMANS 7)

The prophets have spoken. God has come near. By the movement of the Spirit, the promise is here. Receive grace and peace, God's gifts to bring. Go forth to welcome the child! Go forth to receive your king!

DECEMBER 24/DECEMBER 25, 2004

Christmas Eve/Christmas Day

B. J. Beu

COLOR
White

SCRIPTURE READINGS
Isaiah 9:2-7; Psalm 96; Titus 2:11-14; Luke 2:1-20

THEME IDEAS
The theme here is joy, for salvation has arrived. Isaiah proclaims joy that the people who walked in darkness have seen a great light. God's glory has been made manifest in the birth of a child who will be called Wonderful Counselor, Mighty God, Everlasting Father, Prince of Peace. God's justice shall be established forever, and the world will be a place of righteousness. The Epistle and Gospel readings identify this child as God's Son, Jesus Christ. Hear the good news. Christ is born. In Christ, we find the fulfillment of our Advent expectations: peace, hope, love, and joy.

CALL TO WORSHIP (PSALM 96)
O Sing to the Lord a new song.
Sing to the Lord, all the earth!
Declare God's glory among the nations.
Proclaim God's salvation to all people.

For great is the Lord,
and greatly to be praised.
O Sing to the Lord a new song.
Sing to the Lord, all the earth!

CALL TO WORSHIP (LUKE 2)

Sing, choirs of angels.
Sing, you heavenly hosts.
Rejoice, you shepherds in the fields.
Leave your flocks and worship the newborn king.
Salvation is at hand.
Heaven has come down to earth.
Sing, choirs of angels.
Sing, you heavenly hosts.

CONTEMPORARY GATHERING WORDS (PSALM 96)

Sing to the Lord a new song.
We sing of our salvation.
Sing to the Lord a new song.
The Lord is coming.
Sing to the Lord.

CONTEMPORARY GATHERING WORDS (ISAIAH 9)

Walk no longer in darkness. The light of the world has come.
The Christ child is with us. Our salvation is at hand.
Give glory to the One who is worthy to be praised:
Wonderful Counselor, Mighty God, Everlasting Father, Prince of Peace.

PRAISE SENTENCES (LUKE 2)

Glory to God in the highest! Christ is born! Let earth receive her King! Glory to God in the highest!

PRAISE SENTENCES (ISAIAH 2)

Praise God's holy name! Praise the One who is called:
Wonderful Counselor, Mighty God, Everlasting Father,
Prince of Peace. Praise God's holy name!

OPENING PRAYER (ISAIAH 2, LUKE 2)

God of light and glory, we come to you with hope and joy
in our hearts. Help us to walk in darkness no longer. Be
our true light, that we may be instruments of your justice
and peace. Guide our steps to the manger, that we may
behold your gift of salvation, in the life of our Lord. We
ask this in the name of the child born for us: Wonderful
Counselor, Mighty God, Everlasting Father, Prince of
Peace. Amen.

OPENING PRAYER (LUKE 2)

God of love,
    choirs of angels sang to your glory
    on the night your Son was born.
Loosen our tongues,
    that we too may join their heavenly song.
Help us follow the shepherds,
    leaving our cares behind us
as we behold your glory
on this most holy of nights.
May our worship be fitting for the One
    who is the Lord of Life. Amen.

BENEDICTION (ISAIAH 9, LUKE 2)

Walk in darkness no longer.
    We will walk in the light of Christ.
Sing of Christ's birth with the choirs of angels.
    We will sing with the heavenly hosts.
Go and proclaim the good news, Jesus Christ is born.

BENEDICTION (TITUS 2)

God's grace has been given to us,
   bringing salvation to all.
God's grace has been given to us,
   that we might lead godly lives.
God's grace has been given to us,
   that we might become servants of those in need.
Amen.

DECEMBER 26, 2004

First Sunday After Christmas
Mary J. Scifres

COLOR
White

SCRIPTURE READINGS
Isaiah 63:7-9; Psalm 148; Hebrews 2:10-18; Matthew 2:13-23

THEME IDEAS
The Howard Thurman poem "When the Song of the Angels Is Stilled," which inspired the Jim Strathdee song "I Am the Light of the World," always comes to mind after Christmas. Today's readings are vivid reminders that even the presence of God in our world does not eliminate cruelty and oppression. Suffering is all around us, even when the Christ child is in our very midst. Perhaps the most important message we can take away from each Christmas season is the reminder that we are called to follow the One who suffered and loved even those who inflicted that suffering.

CALL TO WORSHIP (PSALM 148, MATTHEW 2)
Praise the Holy One!
Even when children are suffering?
Praise the God of heaven and earth!
Even when God seems so far away?

Praise the One who commands and creates.
Even when goodness seems so powerless?
Praise the One whose glory is above earth and heaven.
Even when we cannot see that glory?
In praising God, we laugh at the oppressor!
Praise the Holy One!
In praising God, we bring Christ into our midst.
Praise the Christ Child!
In praising the Holy One, we create a world of love and joy.
Praise God, whose goodness is stronger than evil!
Praise God, whose glory is above heaven and earth.

CALL TO WORSHIP (PSALM 148)

Praise our God, Yahweh!
Praise God from the heavens and the highest places!
Praise our Lord, Adonai!
Praise God with the angels and heavenly host.
Praise God on High.
Praise God with the sun, the moon, and the stars.
Praise the One who rules the earth.
Praise God with snow and frost, wind and storm.
Praise the name of Yahweh!
For God is always with us. Praise God!

CONTEMPORARY GATHERING WORDS (PSALM 148)

Praise God from the heavens.
Praise God!
Praise God in the heights.
Praise God!
Praise God from the earth.
Praise God!
Praise God from the depths below.
Praise God!

Praise God, young and old, man and woman, ruler and servant.
Praise God!

PRAISE SENTENCES (PSALM 148)

Praise the Lord! Praise the Lord! Praise the Lord!

PRAISE SENTENCES (CHRISTMAS)

Christ is born. Alleluia! Christ is born. Alleluia!

OPENING PRAYER (CHRISTMAS)

Christ Child, Holy One of Bethlehem,
    we come into your presence this day
    to thank you for blessing us,
    and for being our true Christmas gift.
Let your presence flow over our worship,
    that we might know the gift of your spirit,
    and be emboldened to share it
    with all those we meet.
Amen.

PRAYER OF THANKSGIVING

Loving God, we thank you for the angels who proclaimed your birth and saved your life. We thank you for the messengers who even today proclaim your birth and save our lives. We thank you for your guiding light, even in the darkest of life's seasons. Your gracious deeds are all around us, blessing us on this journey. With gratitude, we pray in your Holy Name. Amen.

BENEDICTION

As you go forth, take the song of the angels with you.
We go forth, singing Christ's story for all the earth to hear.
Let the Spirit of Christmas guide you, in the days and weeks and year ahead.
We leave this place, taking the Spirit with us.

CONTRIBUTORS LIST

ERIK ALSGAARD
Father of Zach and Sarah, is the editor of *Newscope* and *FaithLink*.

LAURA JAQUITH BARTLETT
Serves as minister of music in the Oregon-Idaho Conference of The United Methodist Church, where she also spends time as a leader in outdoor ministry, raising two daughters, and learning to play the djembe.

ROBERT BLEZARD
Is an author and editor for the Evangelical Lutheran Church of America.

CHRISTINE BOARDMAN
was a professional singer in her former career and now specializes in interim judicatory ministry in the United Church of Christ.

MARY BOYD
Is pastor of Coupeville United Methodist Church on Whidbey Island, Washington. Also an archaeologist and

textile artist, she shares a household with her husband, son, and three cats.

JOHN BREWER

Has been in ministry for more than thirty years, served as a United Methodist District Superintendent for eight years and dean of the cabinet for two. Even so, he still remembers how to write beautifully for worship! He is married with three children and four grandchildren, and enjoys biking and golfing.

JOANNE CARLSON BROWN

Is a United Methodist minister with a foot in two worlds of parish (pastor of United Church in University Place—a United Church of Christ-United Methodist Church joint congregation) and academia (adjunct Professor at Seattle University). She finds her inspiration in her furperson, Ceilidh, the wonder Westie.

MELANIE LEE CAREY

Plays multiple roles of mom, wife, local church pastor, friend, cook, and bottle-washer.

ROGER C. DOWDY

A United Methodist pastor, is founder of CROSS-PATHS Ministries, a consulting and worship ministry in Richmond, Virginia. You may contact him at (804) 754-8371 or through the Internet: www.CrossPathsMinistries.com.

JOEL EMERSON

Works and serves in Nashville, Tennessee.

REBECCA GAUDINO

Is a United Church of Christ pastor in Portland, Oregon.

PHIL HARRINGTON
Is a United Methodist pastor in the Pacific Northwest and claims that his Wesleyan Methodist roots, Mennonite training, and the influence of his Catholic friends have helped make him the pastor he is today.

NANCY CRAWFORD HOLM
Received her Master of Arts in Pastoral Studies from Seattle University and is currently a Doctoral Candidate in Change Agent studies. She works as an artist and musician, as well as a private A.D.D. coach.

HANS HOLZNAGEL
Is a layman and author, serving the United Church of Christ in Cleveland.

BILL HOPPE
Is a musician and a friend of Aslan. (He also plays piano and plans worship with the planning team at Bear Creek United Methodist Church in Woodinville, Washington.)

CARLA IRIS
Is a poet, musician, and active United Methodist laywoman in Michigan.

SARAH KALISH
Is a graduate of Boston University School of Theology and a United Methodist pastor, serving in North Carolina.

SARA LAMBERT
Loves God and her family, and enjoys sharing music, shepherding youth, exploring creativity, and playing with friends.

LINDA LEE
Is Resident Bishop of the Michigan Area of the United Methodist Church.

SHERRY PARKER
Pastors Dundee United Methodist Church in Michigan.

JUDY SCHULTZ
Pastors Crown Hill United Methodist Church in Seattle.

DON SHIPLEY
Is one of the pastors at Olympia United Methodist Church in Washington.

BEA BARBARA SOOTS
Is the pastor of Redford United Methodist Church, outside of Detroit, and continues to serve her parishes with a strong call to prophetic ministries of social justice.

MARK W. STAMM
Is Assistant Professor of Christian Worship at Perkins School of Theology in Dallas, Texas.

KIRSI STJERNA
A native Finn and mother of two wonderful children, is rostered in the Evangelical Lutheran Church of America. She currently serves as Assistant Professor of Reformation Church History and Director of the Institute for Luther Studies at Lutheran Theological Seminary at Gettysburg.

BRENDA TUDOR
Serves Centenary United Methodist Church and other churches in Spokane, Washington, by combining social jus-

tice preaching and teaching with community development activism.

LAWRENCE A. (LARRY) WIK

Is a United Methodist pastor and an active musician. With his wife Jennifer, he parents three young children.

BRIAN WREN

Is a hymnwriter, minister of the United Reformed Church (UK), and professor of worship at Columbia Theological Seminary.

SCRIPTURE INDEX